# SHORTHAND LETTERS OF SAMUEL PEPYS

PHOTOGRAPH OF FOLIO 139

showing the conclusion of Letter IX and the whole of Letter X. The long-hand words *Guyland*, *Dog* and *Baterton* can be clearly seen.

# SHORTHAND LETTERS OF SAMUEL PEPYS

From a volume entitled
*S. Pepys' Official Correspondence 1662-1679*

Transcribed & edited by
EDWIN CHAPPELL

CAMBRIDGE
AT THE UNIVERSITY PRESS
1933

## CAMBRIDGE
### UNIVERSITY PRESS

University Printing House, Cambridge CB2 8BS, United Kingdom

Cambridge University Press is part of the University of Cambridge.

It furthers the University's mission by disseminating knowledge in the pursuit of
education, learning and research at the highest international levels of excellence.

www.cambridge.org
Information on this title: www.cambridge.org/9781107585959

© Cambridge University Press 1933

First published 1933
First paperback edition 2015

*A catalogue record for this publication is available from the British Library*

ISBN 978-1-107-58595-9 Paperback

# CONTENTS

# INTRODUCTION

It is by this time common knowledge that nearly all Samuel Pepys' books and manuscripts passed in 1724, after the death of his nephew John Jackson, into the keeping of Magdalene College, Cambridge. A few books, however, including five volumes of letters, remained in the private ownership of the Pepys-Cockerell family until 1931, when they were sold by auction. As the result of this sale, one of these volumes of letters, with the misleading title, *S. Pepys' Official Correspondence 1662–1679*, came into the possession of the Trustees of the National Maritime Museum. It is a folio volume of 898 pages containing about 940 letters, memoranda, etc., of which 45 are wholly, and 11 partly in shorthand. It is hoped that eventually every one of these documents will be published, but as the editing of the whole 940 would have meant considerable delay, it was thought that the public demand would be better satisfied with a preliminary selection. Some of the longhand letters have already been printed, wholly or in part, in *Further Correspondence of Samuel Pepys 1662–1679*, edited by the late Dr J. R. Tanner. In his Introduction to that book, he makes the following remark: 'In making the selection printed in this volume, it has been necessary to omit a good many letters of a routine character, but the editor thinks he may claim that everything of historical or biographical importance has been included'. This of course was not intended to include the shorthand letters, which at that time had not been transcribed. It seemed therefore a natural proceeding to take Dr Tanner at his word, for the time being, and to supplement his selection with the transcribed shorthand letters in full, leaving only, what he considered, the less important longhand letters for publication at a later date. While it is believed to be true that the shorthand letters have not been transcribed, it must not be overlooked that their original longhand counterparts may still be in existence. This is known to be so in the case of three letters to Lord Sandwich concerning the Prize-Goods Scandal. (Nos. 34, 35, 39.) A few sentences from these letters are quoted by Mr F. R. Harris in his *Life of Edward Mountagu, first Earl of Sandwich*, and two of them are printed in full in the *Occasional Papers* of the Pepys Club. The longhand originals are in the possession of the present Earl of Sandwich.

Astonishment is often expressed that Pepys' Diary remained untranscribed for a hundred and twenty years after his death, but the extraordinary want of curiosity that this denoted, is as nothing compared with that which allowed these letters to wait yet another hundred years after Pepys and his Diary had become household words, in spite of the fact that their existence was well known.

It is impossible to be consistent in spelling without modernising the longhand of the original, as several clerks, besides Pepys himself, held greatly diverging views on this matter, which seems to have been of very slight importance in the seventeenth century. There could be no question of imitating any one of these spellings for the transcription of the shorthand, and so the decision has been made to render the shorthand in modern spelling in Roman type, and the original longhand in the actual spelling in Italics, with the exception that contractions (e.g. l̄r̄e for letter), initials of persons (e.g. Sir W. P. for Sir Wm. Penn) and perversions of place-names (e.g. Quinsborough for Königsberg) have been expanded and modernised. This has been done chiefly with a view of making the text comprehensible without irritating the reader by a plethora of foot-notes. For the same reason, where necessary an explanatory note precedes each letter.

One would like to think that it is unnecessary at this time to expose the old heresy that Pepys wrote his Diary in a secret cipher, which one writer improved by the addition of the words 'of his own invention', but it seems necessary to state the truth yet once more.

A cipher is a system of secret writing that is intended to be unintelligible to all but those who hold the key and, with this end in view, it is only natural that the number of such persons should be very limited. A system of shorthand is a means of rapid writing, and has no aims at secrecy at all; on the contrary, its author is often a commercially minded person who wishes to sell as many copies of his work as possible. These two clearly differentiated objects should show the error made by interchanging the words 'cipher' and 'shorthand'. Pepys did not write his Diary or these letters in a cipher at all, but in a very popular system of shorthand, invented by Thomas Shelton.

This author seems to have produced a system about the year 1620, which was superseded in 1641 by an improved one with the name of *Tachygraphy*; this went through numerous editions, one being printed at the University Press, Cambridge, in 1645, the copy in the Pepysian Library being dated 1691. In an age when carbon copies and even copying-presses were unknown, there must have been a great demand for anything that would lighten the labour of writing, and a system that had been in print for fifty years must have been known to as large a proportion of the clerical population of those days, as that to which Pitman's shorthand is to-day. It is definitely stated in the Diary that both Hewer and Sir Wm. Coventry were familiar with the system, so that it is quite contrary to the facts to describe it as a cipher. In 1820, the conditions were temporarily different. Shelton's works apparently did not give him immortality, so that when it was first decided to transcribe Pepys' Diary, 'deciphering' was a correct description of the process. When it was discovered later what the system was, and that there was a copy of it in the Pepysian Library, and many copies of it in the British Museum, it again became inaccurate to speak of 'deciphering', 'transcribing' being the correct word to describe what has been done to the present letters.

If *Tachygraphy* was an improvement on its author's previous system, as well as on other systems dating back to 1588, or even earlier, they must have been very poor systems indeed. Shelton may be entitled to the honour given to pioneers, but not on account of the intrinsic excellence of his shorthand. It has several defects: awkward forms, ambiguous signs and undue straggling. It consists of an alphabet of consonants and initial vowels. A final vowel is indicated by a dot in one of five positions, and a medial vowel by the relative positions of the two consonants between which it occurs, such consonants being unjoined. After the alphabet has been learnt, there are lists of prefixes and suffixes, which have little or no connection with the alphabetical signs which they include (e.g. the alphabetical rendering of 'kl' is not only the arbitrary sign for 'it', but also for the suffix '-fication'). The learner's task concludes with a long list of arbitrary signs for common words that must be learnt by heart. A necessary sequel to writing shorthand is transcribing it, and in this respect Shelton gave his followers many puzzles to solve, and seems to glory in so doing, for when discussing the resemblance of characters, as in the 'kl' example above, he says: "The same Character sometimes standeth for two things: as for example, there is the same for *-ture* and *Christ*, *-ternal* and *which*, *mess-* and *what*, which is no hindrance (*but a help*)".

It is impossible to indicate the length of the vowels; *stripped* and *striped*, *behalf* and *behave*, *on one* and *own*, are indistinguishable. It is almost impossible to distinguish with certainty: *your* and *great*, *go* and *give*, *work* and *word*, *will* and *answer*, *breadth* and *width*, *they* and *not*, *thou though through* and *thought*, *present* and *promise*. Certain signs are almost laughable, such as those for *carpenter*, *congratulate* and *reimbursed*, all of which could be written as quickly in longhand. It will be seen in the letters that Pepys often writes *carpenter* in longhand, in preference to the unwieldy shorthand. Finally, the punctuation is a difficulty. Pepys only uses one stop sign that has to do duty for all. It is used very sparingly and usually has the value of a full stop, commas being very seldom indicated.

From these remarks it is to be inferred that no claim is made for finality in the transcriptions which follow. Both words and punctuation may be wrong in places, but it is thought that in every letter there is sufficient beyond doubt to make the meaning clear. A few meaningless sentences have been included as giving the reader the best idea of certain corrupt passages and with the hope that suggestions will be made for their elucidation. A few words have baffled all attempts at transcription. In spite of some writers' references to Pepys' beautiful penmanship, the truth is that much of his handwriting is only with difficulty legible, so that in reading the letters, it must not be assumed that the longhand is not subject to revision, on the contrary the longhand has, if anything, caused more trouble than the shorthand.

The folio numbers refer to the pencilled pagination of the original.

As the date of the first letter is 1664 Sept. 20 and of the last 1668 March 30, they all come within the Diary period. It seems most unlikely that anyone who has not read the Diary will read these letters, so that it should be unnecessary to give biographical notes of persons who have already been made familiar in its pages, such as Pepys' fellow members of the Navy Board.

The period covered is also roughly that of the Second Dutch War, to which there are many allusions. The subjects referred to are somewhat diverse. The supply of stores is perhaps the most frequent topic. Appointments, recommendations, hiring of ships, victualling, prize-goods and convoys receive considerable attention, and there are single references to: Prince Rupert's right to wear a standard; the excessive draught of the *Royal Katherine*; the revision of Deane's design for the *Rupert*; the Board's (or Pepys') reproof of Commissioner Pett in reply to his accusation about masts; the name of the most suitable person for the position of Surveyor-General of Victualling; an interview with a woman, an alleged trafficker in tickets; paper, pens, candles and fire for Commissioner Taylor; and lastly, the 'fowle' accusations of Mr Waltham against Mr Lanyon.

E. C.

Greenwich
*November* 1932

# LIST OF WORKS QUOTED

The Diary of Samuel Pepys, M.A., F.R.S.
> Edited by H. B. WHEATLEY. (George Bell & Sons.)
> 1893–9.

Further Correspondence of Samuel Pepys 1662–1679.
> Edited by J. R. TANNER. (George Bell & Sons.) 1929.

The Life, Journals and Correspondence of Samuel Pepys, Esq., F.R.S.
> Deciphered by the REV. JOHN SMITH, A.M. (Out of print.) 1841.

A Descriptive Catalogue of the Naval MSS. in the Pepysian Library.
> Edited by J. R. TANNER. (The Navy Records Society.) 1903–23.

Samuel Pepys's Naval Minutes.
> Edited by J. R. TANNER. (The Navy Records Society.) 1926.

The Historical MSS. Commission, Fifteenth Report, Appendix Part II.
> (H.M. Stationery Office.) 1897.

Occasional Papers. Vol. II, 1917–1923.
> Read by members at meetings. (The Pepys Club.) 1925.

The Life of Edward Mountagu, K.G., first Earl of Sandwich.
> By F. R. HARRIS. (John Murray.) 1912.

Calendar of State Papers. Domestic.

Letters and the Second Diary of Samuel Pepys.
> Edited by R. G. HOWARTH. (J. M. Dent & Sons Ltd.) 1932.

LETTER I                    (f. 110)

¶ The first part of this letter is in longhand, and to that extent has
been printed in *Further Correspondence*. The delicate matter of the
flags was referred to the King for his personal decision. The result
is given on p. 28 of *Further Correspondence*:

"It is determined that the Prince shall carry the flag of union only,
and not that, the King or his Royal Highness being on board."

The revelation may partly clear up an entry in *Pepys' Naval
Minutes*, p. 77:

"No method ever established about the flag for distinguishing the
King's ships of war from his subjects' till I provided a proclamation
for that purpose. Consider Serjeant Knight's Discourse about the
Flag of England. Recollect the disorders and abuses about putting
up the King's flag or Jack, and the particular instances of my oppos-
ing it in the case of the Prince and my Lord Dumblaine."

*May it please your Lordshipp*

*The winde continuing for some days N.E. hath hindred
our Guinea ships from falling downe, which (had the Dutch
fleet beene ready) might have beene of sound advantage to
them, but they are not nor like to bee (as 'tis sayd) in some
days. 'Tis discoursed alsoe as if they were now lesse keen
upon't then they were and talk of new Treatys, nay wagers I
heard offered this day upon the 'Change that noe Dutch fleet
shall attempt to passe the Channell this 3 weeks (meaning
towards Guinea) the ground of which presumption I understand not, but doe wish (as well prepared as wee would have
our ships and stores thought to bee) that a tolerable offer of
accomodation from the Dutch bee the worst news wee heare of
these 12 months. The Mary is ordered this day to bee forth-
with manned and victualled for a Channell voyage.*

It has fallen (my Lord) among other talk once or twice

CPS                    I                    I

lately in my company to be asked how it would be ordered when the Prince and your *Lordshipp* shall meet to do right to both for the flag. I have suffered the discourse to pass unminded by myself not knowing what were fit to say in it. If your *Lordshipp* shall instruct me how to behave myself thereon in case I find the question put with design or expectation of my answer to it, I shall do that your *Lordshipp* shall command me.

Yesterday the *Duke* at our attending him enquired what was allowable by custom to the Prince as to the wearing of a standard. It was answered (by the old ones) that no admiral in their memory had ever done it, the standard implying the King's being present at least, no higher signal of the King's presence is provided than it. But his being of the blood *Royall* rendering his case different from that of any admiral in memory (excepting his present Highness) they knew not what to determine and so left it to have the King's pleasure known in it.

*May it please your Lordshipp*
*Your Lordshipp's obedient Servant*
*S. P.*

*Lord Sandwich at Portsmouth.*
*Sept. 20th. 1664.*

## LETTER II

❡ War with the Dutch seemed imminent, the Duke of York had gone to sea, taking with him Mr Coventry as Secretary and Sir William Penn as Commander. The 'Lords' referred to in the last paragraph were 'The Committee of the Lords for the Navy' mentioned in the Diary on 1664 Nov. 11, who acted for the Duke of York in his absence. Sir William Warren, the timber merchant, was at one time a very great friend of Pepys, until he became 'great with my Lord Brouncker' so that Pepys dare not trust him as he used to do.

2

*Sir*

I have received yours of the 17th., and am not only confirmed from you but by advertisement this day from *Capt. Fortescue* of the condition of his ship (which till then I knew not of but from your former letter) so that I will to-morrow night send for him overland being in hopes then to do more myself as well as understand better what others do. Pray let some directions from you meet him here.

The enclosed will tell you the proceedings of *Sir W. Penn* who is well in the *Downes* after much ill weather.

I wish as things are your quantity of deals had been greater though the price be high, the uncertainty of *Sir W. Warren's* and the greater charge of sending supplies from hence making it much to be wished.

I will take care to have a supply of *Ironworke* put on board a small vessel to-morrow, though I cannot force it into the thoughts of others that anything of the great demand needed to be thought of till this fleet be dispatched away which they say has been supplied long ago with everything demanded hence, which (upon calling for the papers this day to examine) I find quite otherwise. I make it not my purpose to charge my letters alway with reflections on others and I hope you do believe me herein, but the care taken of the safety of the King's service (which you ought to know) cannot be told truly without it.

I cannot lack during my little observation in the Navy demonstrations sufficient to evince the truth of your opinion concerning the effect that introducing of *merchants* into the Navy will have and those not general only but special to and some not foreign to persons in nomination, and could therefore wish that it might be deliberated on

3

and freedom allowed to offer what may be said on this subject before a thing of such import to the well doing of this office be concluded on. For my own particular my work *ebbs* and flows not by the number of officers, but by the increase or wane of the public action and so shall be little concerned otherwise than as one that desires a concurrence of everything else to the advancement of that to which he wishes so well in his proper *sphere*.

I omit to give you account of the commands we daily receive from the Lords, believing that you have it from them.

I am Sir

Your most affectionate and humble servant

S. P.

*Mr. Coventry at Portsmouth*
*Nov. 18th. 1664.*

(ff. 125–7)

# LETTER III

[Marginal note] £4-15-00
[This is the price of Castle's knees per load. See next letter]

¶ This long letter is concerned with the provision of stores and the appointment of commissioners for Portsmouth and Harwich. The passage about tobacco-stalks is curious. It seems as though the usual wadding for the guns was unobtainable and Pepys, with much resource, had thought of this strange substitute. Although the gentlemen readily caught at the objection of the smell, in the next letter, after a little reflection apparently, this objection becomes an advantage. In a letter from Sir Wm. Coventry dated 1665 Apr. 15 he promises to send Pepys an account as soon as any experiment is made with tobacco-stalk, but he wishes even leather shavings might be sent down to supply the great want. Although there are other letters in existence concerning tobacco-stalk, which give the impression that the experiment was successful, as late as Aug. 18 nothing seems to have been done, because Col. Middleton writes to

4

Pepys on that date telling him that he will see what can be done with the tobacco-stalks as wadding for guns. (*Cal. S. P. Dom.*) Bolt-ropes are ropes sewn round the edges of sails to strengthen them. Cooper is mentioned again in letter No. 13 as the prospective purveyor at Alice Holt, if he would moderate his demands. 'I would be' should surely read 'It would be', but the shorthand signs for 'I' and 'It' are quite distinct. The remark about Pett is none too clear, but he seems to have made a *volte-face* concerning the necessity for an assistant and then denied that he had done so. The two new commissioners were Col. Middleton for Portsmouth and Capt. Taylor for Harwich. Sir Henry Bennet, afterwards Lord Arlington, was a Secretary of State, and a month or so later, Comptroller to the Commissioners for Prize Goods. Messrs Wood and Castle were timber merchants. Knees are pieces of naturally curved wood, employed in shipbuilding. There were at least three Taylors, and it is not quite clear whose recovery is referred to, but most probably it is Capt. Taylor the timber merchant. It is much to be regretted that we have no record of Sir W. Warren's disingenuous practices. Mr Sheldon was Clerk of the Cheque at Woolwich. It will be remembered that it was to his house that Mrs Pepys went during the Plague. The new Call-books were an invention of Pepys, first referred to in the Diary on 1662 Oct. 24, and put into practice on Dec. 22 of the same year. They are also mentioned in a letter to the Clerk of the Cheque at Deptford which is printed on p. 2 of *Further Correspondence.*

*Sir*

As part of an answer to your *volume* of the 18th. I am sorry to find so much matter of trouble charged on you wishing more might be done here to lessen your care there. For your wish of chain plate along with the blocks and *oares* I have rummaged the market but find that that commodity is provided but upon occasion and if to be had of the common size would not fit the King's use. *Port-hinges* as I think I told you last night are shipped. In *general* as to *Ironworke* I was told that the King's smiths do designedly slacken in their deliveries complaining of the lowering of their prices of late. For remedy whereof (being conscious of the power they as well as others at this time have over us) I went to them with an offer of a liberty of continuing or present resigning their late contract and found them both mighty pliant promising all dispatch to what shall be demanded, which I have this day prepared for them very largely.

More colours shall come this week and the new *mixtures* suddenly staying a little for the dyeing *greene and yellow*.

The *Gentlemen* here do readily catch at the objection of the smell against *Tobacco stalks* but nobody enquires after anything in lieu of it, so that I must either subject myself to the reproof of an *Innovator* in this as in other things or else the fleet must want *wadding* for aught I see.

The sail maker is to bring his answer to-morrow about *Boltropes*.

I have told you in one of my former that we have answered Mr. *Johnson's* demand of £2,000. I last night desired the names of any *Masters* or surgeons neglecting attendance upon which our enquiry shall proceed, the Lords shall be addressed too upon the discovery of any man guilty.

For the *Ropemakers* I will assure you we are made to believe that by two days' work is performed (without abatement for night work) just twice as much work at *Woolwich* as heretofore by a single day's work and no doubt the like is at *Chatham*. We have sent twice for *Capt. Fortescue* and if he be not gone from *Yarmouth* I hope we shall have him here or hear of him to-morrow.

As to *Cooper* I would be (at any time but this) a pleasant observation to see how some words extorted from *Chr. Pett* heretofore (which for telling truth *Deane* became an *offender*) touching the *uselessness* of an *Assistant* there, are *urged* against his demanding an *Assistant* now who so lately declared the little need of any, so that unless *Chr. Pett* solicits the Lords, I do not see he is like to have any, yet without *Question* he must have one now that we are going to build as well as repair, though I am well contented he should hereby learn the use of speaking truth.

*As* to the *Commissioners* for *Portsmouth* and *Harwich*, I told you last night the orders I had received from the Lords on attending the *Attorney General* for new drafts of their commission. I have since done it and (it being corrected upon reading to the *Secretary*) I have caused it to be writ over fair and by directions of *Sir H. Bennet* do send it for his *Royal Highness'* perusal and allowance if he judges it fit. He bid me offer whether the title of *Sub-commissioner* would not best suit their restrained power which as he only proposed it by the by, so I think where their *authority* is so sufficiently *circumscribed*, it would unnecessarily diminish their *authority* in the yards not to be called *Commissioners*.

I gave you last night an account of a passage which has made *Wood* and *Castle's* pretensions fail so as to have *Taylor's recovery* borne very peaceably. As for *Castle's* knees we have a week since bought them, but I must needs say were led to it (though in truth there wanted not a great measure of worth in the very goods to lead us to the price) by one of the most *disingenuous* practices in reference to *Sir W. Warren* that ever was used by one man to another. I won't offend you with the circumstances till I see you (which God send).

There is nothing now but the modesty of the merchant protects us from paying 50/- instead of 25/- for all things we buy, and did you see who the merchants are that begin to haunt us, you would neither judge their modesty any great protection, nor that the protecting of contracts for *Anchors etc.* arised merely from *Supineness.*

Will you please to consider whether a *Clerk* of the *Cheque* will be needful at *Harwich* or no. The officers of *Woolwich* yard have wrote in the commendation of the servant of Mr. *Sheldon* for it. How far I am *bribed* in the cause I will tell you. I did the other day direct him by his *New Callbooks* to compute the charge of the shipwrights' and *calkers'* work of the new ship, which he has since done and as a secret presented me with an account that it amounts to 5500 and *odd* pounds, which (let me tell you) in the estimate of her building was given in but £2200. How your *Portsmouth* new ship is provided I know not, but it is hard I think that the *Anchors* for that at *Woolwich* are not yet made, nor will I doubt be ready these six days. Nor are her *Cables* yet dispatched, there being on *Saturday* last at my being there but 4 perfected for her, and strands laid but for 6 of the supply to come to *Portsmouth* by the *Augustine.* It is true we shall compass about 8 or 10 from the rope makers' yards of the *Towne* and about 12 ton of *Cordage* at the most may be depended upon to be wrought out of hemp in a week which is so far from answering our expense, that I fear we must use other rope grounds though on bad terms. Pray think of it and give me your direction. I shall not be rid of my Lord *Treasurer* these two days which hinders my enlarging now.

I am *Sir*

Your most humble servant

S. P.

Mr. *Coventry*
*Nov.* 22 1664.

8

# LETTER IV (ff.128-30)

¶ This very long letter is concerned with a variety of matters beginning with the hire of a smack, where the meticulous Pepys draws attention to the fact that the contract does not state the kind of month. Light anchors were apparently not made at Bristol. Chr. Pett's recantation again gets mentioned. Boatswains', gunners' and carpenters' mates seem to have been scarce, and a touch of humour is contained in the appointment of 'two of the youngest of the Elder Brethren' to find them. The 12*d.* per man for six months must refer to payment for sick men, as the same rate and persons are mentioned in this connection in letter No. 6. Mr Lewes was assistant to Mr (afterwards Sir Dennis) Gauden, the Victualler of the Navy. Gauden's house at Clapham subsequently became Hewer's, and in it Pepys spent the last two years of his life and died there. Blackburgh was a timber merchant mentioned in the Diary as having made Pepys a fine dinner only to himself. The smell of the tobacco-stalks, far from being an objection as in the previous letter, is now not only pleasant, but healthy. The trouble about the payment of pressed men seems to be that if they were paid from the time of being received on board any ship, instead of from the time of being received on board the ship for which they were intended, it would be difficult to check this date, so that commanders and pursers between them would be able to ante-date their entry into the service for their own profit. The attempt to get the Navy Board made Commissioners for Prizes was not successful because 'the King and the Duke had resolved to put in some Parliament men that have deserved well'. Slop-sellers were clothing contractors. 'Slops', to this day, is a naval term for clothing. 'This being very short' is another of the rare playful touches.

*Sir*

I have received yours of the 22nd. and in it the contract for a *Smacke.* For our times of payment we *covenant* to pay them one month's advance and the rest leave at large, nor are the kinds of months determined (which it may be is an oversight) but as others are, so shall the master of this be used.

*Sir J. Knight* did the other day tell us that lighter than *27 cwt. Anchors* are not made at *Bristoll* and in the consideration we have not proceeded to set any a-making, but being not satisfied with the reason of our not proceeding

9

(*viz.* because they may be made here) I have wrote to know their prices from that size downwards and if below ours in any proportion to pay for their transportation, I shall give you my opinion thereon.

I am sorry that *Dover* holds out so long in her *ill* luck.

*Chr. Pett* has, after many reproofs for his former denying the need of an *Assistant* (though he fixedly denies it), left it to the choice of the Board to allow him one or no, but withal declaring his incapacity to do his work without one. Whereupon the *Gentlemen* concerned *vouching* the truth of his former denial do (rather than stand to the blame may follow the obstruction of the service) choose to suffer and to have one, and therefore you will be pleased to think of one fit for the place among the King's *carpenters*.

I have proposed the want of *Mates* to *Boatswains, Gunners* and *Carpenters*. We have appointed two of the youngest of the Elder *Brethren* of *Trinity* House to look out for a supply of the two latter. But for *Boatswains'* Mates *Sir W. Batten* apprehends they cannot be wanting where so many able seamen are. I must confess for *Gunners'* I can see little, but if I knew about what number of *Carpenters'* Mates would be entertained I do not think but with a little pains a supply of able men might be gathered in the *River*, which as you advise me I will endeavour to have done. *Holly and Ash* shall be minded the next time we attend the Lords.

*Colours* are dyed of *Greene, Yellow and Redd*, to be made up thus to be striped

White and Green     White and Yellow     White and Red

I have ordered three of *each* to be made. If you approve not of it, be pleased to stop us by your next.

I am informed that the *Purser* of the *Happy* Return went yesterday out of town for *Portsmouth*, the reason of his delay I cannot learn, the *victualler* not owning it, nor could I hear at all of him till this day.

The *Sayle maker* says he is very well provided of *Boltropes*. We have directed him to cause to be made at *Portsmouth* (to spare) the sails following:

| Rate | Suits |
|------|-------|
| 1 | 1 |
| 2 | 2 |
| 3 | 3 |
| 4 | 4 |
| 5 | 4 |

As you judge it too much or too little, let us know it.

Your proposal of choosing masters upon vacancies abroad is very well accepted.

Order is taken about the *12d. per man* for *6 months* and Mr. *Lewes* has by our order promised to write to Mr. *Gauden* who is said to be still at *Portsmouth*, to order the paying of it.

I wrote in my report to you the other day that the *Double-day-workers* do twice times as much work as is required for the task of a single day, without an allowance for the night working.

As for *Ironworke*, I am advised that the *Quantity* of port hinges gone are *700 payre* and 380 port hooks and 20 chain plates. I directed the sending of all [that] could be spared, but how this will answer your wants, I know not. Our friends here are of opinion that the smiths of *Gosport* and *Portsmouth* cannot but be able to answer all your occasions of the sort.

*Sir W. Warren* is gone to *Harwich* about his ship of

masts, so I can say nothing of his, but *Blackburgh's* plea for non-delivery of his plank is want of ships, which our refusal to protect their seamen, he says, *occasioned*, but being little satisfied with the excuse, I endeavoured to lay open his danger to him and have his promise of speeding it in a little time, he protesting that it has been ready at the water side a great while. If he do not perform his promise suddenly, some other way shall be thought on for him, and so I told him.

We shall in two vessels hired and the *Augustine* send you *100 Tons* of hemp, some *Tobacco stalkes* shall also come in the *Augustine*. Our friends not agreeing only to it, but saying the smell will rather please than offend and will be healthy too, rather than the contrary.

It is judged here that press men ought to be entered into the King's pay from the time they are received on board any ship though but in order to their transportation else-where, so that we must be contented with the number of tickets it will occasion and the *uncontrollable dates* of the entry of each man, which if the commanders or pursers shall become purchasers of, though small tickets, as likely they must or well may prove very chargeable.

Why more such *Knees* as *Castle's* might not be sent for from *Biscay* I know not, for though I was answered that it cannot be done without a licence there to export them, yet I am well assured Mr. *Castle* has agreed for more by the same man. He has his at £*3-8-0*, so he confesses for which we pay him £*4-15-0 per loade*. Which in our expense were worth saving.

My last brought you the result of the Lords touching *Capt. Taylor* and a new draft of his and *Col. Middleton's* commission.

Upon *Thursday* last *Capt. Cocke* came to the office (*Sir G. Carteret* being there) with an order of the Lords for receipt of £5000 as *Treasurer* for sick and wounded men. This did give occasion to *Sir W. Batten* (whether suddenly or upon deliberation, I know not) to ask *Sir George* whether he thought His *Majesty* might not be prevailed with to give the officers of the Navy the same favour which the *Parliament* did. *Morris, Twiddy* and *Cranly* the then *Commissioners*, to make them *Commissioners* of *Prize Goods. Sir George* very friendlily replied that if he did indeed expect any such thing, it was now the season and he would be willing to promote it. Whereupon *Sir J. Mennes joyned* and though well assured that if my pains be found more than ordinary, I serve too noble a master to doubt being considered, yet, no inconvenience appearing to me upon so tempting a surprise, I fell in too. What *Sir George* will do in it, I know not nor shall be very *sollicitous*, but I thought fit to give you this account of it, that if it should come before you, you might know the reason of it and proceed (without the least regard to me) to favour or remove it, as you judge expedient.

We have a good while since given order to the slop-sellers about the business of clothes to the pressed men, by them to be shown to the *Commanders* of each ship. The copy of it I have enclosed, not to obstruct the having it done more amply by His *Royal Highness*. This being very short

*Sir, I am*

Your most faithful servant

*S. P.*

*Mr. Coventry*
*Nov.* 24 1664.

¶ Mr Tippets (afterwards Sir John) was at this time Master Shipwright at Portsmouth. Later, he was a commissioner and Surveyor
of the Navy. One of the stenographic puzzles is the object kept by
the keeper who should have his allowance. The shorthand sign is
most clearly written, and should be either 'gap' or 'pug'. 'Unnecessariness' is a word which rather aptly describes itself. Ham-
maccoes are merely hammocks and not as stated by Wheatley in his
note to his edition of the Diary on 1664/5 Feb. 21.

*Sir*

I have yours of the 23rd. I have communicated it to
the Board and a contract is made for a good supply of
those *Ironworks* you therein mention. Mr. *Tippetts* is wrote
to about the dimensions of the new ship's furnaces. Your
reasons for delaying the launching of it are judged very
well laid together. What *Elm* plank or board can be found
that may be served into the yard shall be suddenly sent
thither. The [gap?] keeper will have an order for his
allowance as others have. *Sir W. Warren* is since come
back and assures us that he has a ship actually loaded with
deals and designed for *Portsmouth* and now upon her way.
We are made to believe that the like despatch is made at
*Chatham* and *Woolwich* rope grounds which you speak of,
but reckoning the times and time taken up in laying the
cables we are bid not to expect above 12 tons to be per-
fectly wrought up in a week, one week with another,
which is but a small proportion to our expense and to see
how the rope makers and others swarm about us with
little tenders of 10 or 12 tons at a time of their cordage
and yet (*such* as the quality and price of it is) how we
are forced to receive them without finding fault, is a sad
contemplation.

I have discoursed with the slop-sellers and find them
ready to send good quantities presently, though they say

they hear not from their correspondent of any great wants, but this they say, that the *Duke's* late warrant obliging them to issue no further than the wages of the men grow due, either the men must want clothes till a month be out or more, or else they must trust them at their adventure if the men should die or run away before the value of their clothes arises in their wages. I must confess I apprehended your meaning and the Board's (while you were with us) to have been that the men should have two months' credit upon their future service, and accordingly drew up our warrant. Be pleased to consider whether it will not be necessary to credit the press men a little further than the *Duke's* warrant seems to intend. They further say that beds without assurance of a vend must not be over plentifully laid into ships, they being the dearest commodity and the aptest to suffer of any they deal for, and therefore would be glad to be instructed about what quantities we expect, but rugs, waistcoats, drawers (and coats if they might be suffered) they are ready to send good quantities of, and will the next week.

The *Rosebush* is not yet gone. I sent for *Baker*, he says she shall sail on *Monday* next, the wind permitting.

For the title of *Sub-commissioner* I think I did give you my thoughts of its unnecessariness. The Lords have not met since the Parliament (at least I have not had notice of it) so that till Monday I shall not know their resolution as to that of the *subordinary* of the two *extra-Commissioners* to the ordinary. Pray let me hear whether you do think of a convoy for *Tangier* against the 10th. of *December*, or what you would have done in it. The Lords have ordered us to prepare some store of *Masts etc.* to be sent to *Dover*. Be pleased to advise what is expedient to be done thereon and how far it is necessary to set up a factory there. About 2,000 *Hamaccoes* are sent away this week for *Portsmouth* and a good supply more shall be going the next. My next shall give you an account of the state of the naval charge, as we have lately reported it.

*Sir, I am*

Your most humble servant

S. P.

*Mr. Coventry*
*Nov.* 26 1664.

## LETTER VI

❡ The reference to colours evidently arises from Coventry's answer concerning the flags sketched in letter No. 4. Messrs Gauden and Lewes and the 12*d.* per sick man were also mentioned in that letter. Col. Middleton, again, was the Commissioner-elect for Portsmouth. The proposal of Sir W. Batten may have been the Prize Office suggestion of letter No. 4. Capt. Tinker was Master-Attendant at Deptford and Capt. Lancaster seems to have been employed in some capacity in Portsmouth yard, but no explanation can be offered as to the relation of one to the other, nor of Lancaster's removal. The postscript with its interpolated memorandum is interesting. Capt. Taylor was a 'fanatique' but 'a man of great abilities and despatch'; as the former, he was not acceptable to the Lords; and as the latter, he was acceptable to the Duke of York. The Lords' mild effrontery towards the Duke is perhaps one of the earliest acts of hostility which, eight years later, culminated in the Test Act; and twenty-four years later, in the Revolution.

*Sir*

Yours of the 26th. I have. It was my willingness to comply with your direction (that the *colours* last ordered should be *striped*) and my not hearing of any better fashions for them, that made me choose them I sent you, but (if they please in other regards) the difference in price is not considerable. Having done my part in getting money imprested to Mr. *Gauden* for the 12*d. per* sick man and satisfaction given to Mr. *Lewes* that it should be presently paid, I depended upon Mr. *Lewes'* promise for the signifying this to Mr. *Gauden* that night. He also assured us that the money should be presently paid at *Portsmouth*. I have since spoken with him and have his word that he had done it and that Mr. *Gauden* has since answered that he was taking care in it.

I shall not fail in my careful corresponding with *Col. Middleton* asking your pardon that I did not of myself consider the reasons of your directing me to it.

*Sir* I do most heartily acknowledge the many instances you give me of your real favour and particularly in your advice touching the proposal of *Sir W. Batten's* which I shall duly observe.

It was very *earely* (methinks) for *Capt. Tinker* to demand an *Assistant* and makes me fear that having of the King's work better done will neither be found the cause nor the effect of *Capt. Lancaster's* removal.

Another *Standard* is providing for the *Charles*, and a convoy shall be (the Lords having ordered it) appointed for the *Augustine*.

I assure you I labour all I can for the stocking of *Portsmouth* with stores of all sorts, being very full of the necessity of it.

*Sir* I do most fervently pray to God for your particular safety, and rest

Your faithful and most humble servant

*S. P.*

*The Commissions* are approved of in the manner you see them, with a clause for inferiors to be obedient. *My Lord Lauderdale* being there at the reading of them, demanded how *Taylor* came to be continued. *Secretary Bennet* replied by His *Royal Highness'* answer that he would not alter his choice, whereupon it was moved (for my memory sake it is fit I set down here, that it was *Sir G. Carteret* that moved it, which *Sir J. Mennes* and *Sir W. Batten* must witness for they were there with me then) that it might be entered that the commissionating of *Taylor* was not by the choice of the *Board*, but by order of His *Royal Highness*, which was agreed to accordingly.

*Mr. Coventry*
*Nov.* 29 1664.

(f. 133)                      LETTER VII

¶ This is presumably the letter referred to in the second paragraph of letter No. 6.

*Sir*

I am by the necessity of His *Majesty's* service, Mr. *Coventry's* command and my own inclination triply obliged to *aske* your correspondence and offer mine, with a further tender of whatever services I can do that may signify my particular regards to yourself.

We are at present (in reference to *Portsmouth*) busied in the providing such stores as have been demanded from the officers there for supply of the place, part whereof is despatching in the *Augustine* of which you shall have an invoice speedily, but *Sir*, for as much as through the great hurry we have lately been in, and the great *consumption* withal of His *Majesty's* stores, both there and here, we have not (I fear) before us a right state of the condition of

18

the stores at Portsmouth, so as to be enabled to make a due provision of supplies. I do by the advice of Mr. *Coventry* recommend to you as a matter principally to be regarded that the *Demands* formerly made from the *store keeper* may be presented to you with an account which of them has been answered (which I fear are but few) and that thereupon you would please to direct the drawing up a new and plentiful demand of all provisions to be furnished from hence, which will be of great use for us at all time to *recurre* to, and I shall make it my care to see as amply and seasonably answered as the market and weather will admit.

I will not enter into the discourse of any particulars now, deferring them till I have more time to write and you to read, which (after the going out of the fleet) I hope shall soon be to us both.

One thing only I shall take the liberty to add upon my being advertised that one Mr. *Shales* has made his tenders of serving you as a *clerk*, which is that by the concurrent report of all that know him in his relation to this office, and a very good knowledge I have of him myself, I do esteem him qualified for your use both for integrity, diligence and ability, inferior to no clerk in the *Navy* and one that I am well assured if you entertain him, will be found no less satisfactory to yourself than serviceable to the King in his ready execution of your commands. So wishing you full content in your present station, I rest

Your affectionate friend and servant

*S. P.*

*Col. Middleton*
*Nov.* 29 1664.

❡ The semblance of a victory referred to in the first paragraph was not the result of a fight, but of the Dutch refusing one.

*May it please your Lordshipp*

I do congratulate your *Lordshipp* with your return to *Portsmouth* so much like a victory, your enemy fleeing, but could be glad to apprehend more reason than I yet do of the inference the World generally draws from it, to the questioning the courage or capacity of the *Dutch* to have stood you. However, it is concluded (I find) from their drawing home that they must be beaten unless the King of *France* helps them by *armes and Mediation* and that is the present discourse of the town.

The *Parliament* has been very much divided touching the manner of raising this £2,500,000 and the *honour* of the *vote* much diminished by it, but I think it is well over, by rejecting the (*abhorred*) title of *Tax* and accepting the verity of its method with the name of *Subsidy*. *His Majesty* had his reasons (no question) for preferring this sum payable in 3 years, rather than the offer of a less sum in less time, but having had the single stating of the charge of the Navy to the King and my Lord *Treasurer* upon this occasion, I am well able to say that this sum will not support the *warr* two years and a half, and how welcome the advancing more money will be after the difficulty of raising this your *Lordshipp* may be pleased to consider, besides the *Parliament* being obliged to revoke their word to the *People* for easing them of further charge for three years. Your *Lordshipp's* family is in health, which God preserve to your *Lordshipp*.

I am your *Lordshipp's* most obedient servant

*Lord Sandwich at Portsmouth.*                    *S. P.*
*Dec.* 3rd. 1664.

¶ Mr Young was a flag maker mentioned in the Diary. The return
of the Duke of York and Mr Coventry was from the fleet, their
departure having been referred to in the note to letter No. 2. The
whole fleet seems to have returned to Portsmouth after the Dutch
withdrawal, as the Duke and Coventry came to town from there,
in the previous letter it was seen that Sandwich had returned there,
and the present letter is addressed to Sir Wm. Penn there. The last
paragraph but one is perhaps the most cryptic passage of these letters.
Guyland (an Anglicised form of Ghailán) was a Moorish pretender
who caused us much trouble at Tangier. Taken by itself, no explanation can be offered as to why his health should be considered
good news with which to greet Sir Wm. Penn on his return to harbour. Taken in connection with the following remark about Mrs
Pepys (the only reference to her in these letters) and her dog
Baterton, the suggestion is made that Guyland was some animal of
Penn's, perhaps a monkey, and that as Pepys and he had neighbour-
ing official residences, Pepys would be able to give him this news
from home. The most fitting answer to the question why Mrs Pepys
could not be believed without a visit of inspection, is 'God wot'.
Guyland, Dog and Baterton are all in longhand and beyond any
question. A little doubt was felt at first on transcribing 'God wot',
but less than four months later this phrase occurs in the Diary
(1665 Mar. 28) and thirty years later it is again used. (*Naval
Minutes*, p. 293.)

*Sir*

The enclosed concerns the want of clothes, in answer
to your letter of advice of the *2nd. current. Standards* are
in hand and will be soon despatched, so Mr. *Young* tells
me. There will come by Monday's waggon our flags of
red and white, green and white, and yellow and white, of
forms directed by Mr. *Coventry*, three of each mixture.

We are in hopes of Mr. *Coventry's* being in town to-
night with the *Duke*, and could wish to do the same for
you.

I congratulate you your *triumphant* return, hoping at
least for this advantage by it, that from the many instances
of our unpreparedness before, we may against next time

know how to fit ourselves better in all points, which use I wish with all my heart we may make of it.

For matters relating to the *Dock* I have and shall correspond with *Commissioner Middleton*, with whom I could wish (if your health and business will give leave) you would please to advise about a *round* demand of stores of all sorts, but more particularly of such things I have this night wrote to him about, because there is reason for our speedy looking out for contracts for them.

All's well with *Guyland* and my wife tells me as much of her *Dog Baterton, but* I am fain to believe her without going to see. God wot.

The *Parliament* is resolved to have the *Dutch* beaten whether they will fight or no, so *liberall* they are; but let me entreat you the next time you go out to see that a little *mischiefe* be done for our good friend *Capt. Cocke's* sake, paymaster to the *Sick and Wounded.*

Sir, I am with all my heart

Your humble servant

S. P.

*Sir Wm. Penn at Portsmouth.*
[n.d.]

# LETTER X

⁋ Mr Johnson was the Admiralty agent at Yarmouth.

*Sir*

I doubt not mine is come to hand which told you of my giving compliance to your last desire of a bill of £2,000 which is sent to *Alderman Backwell.*

What small parcel of ropes you shall hereafter collect you will please to send to *Deptford.*

For your *Question* about *Dutch* ships we are here

22

unempowered to give you any advice thereon, but refer you to Mr. *Coventry* who came to town last night and will be ready to signify how His *Royal Highness* directs your proceedings shall be in that matter. *Sir,* I have given him an account of your continued care to serve the King and my endeavours to give due respect to your desires in his absence.

I am

Your very ready friend and servant

*S. P.*

*Mr. Johnson of Yarmouth*
*Dec. 6th.* 1664.

## LETTER XI

¶ It is not known what the enclosure was. The amusement caused by a matter that could be both a great disappointment and some reproach might be explained by the fact that the *Royal Katherine* had been built by Christopher Pett, of whom Pepys had no great opinion, but it seems more likely that 'amused' has its older meaning of 'bewildered'.

*May it please your Lordshipp*

*This principally is to give cover to the enclosed and ask pardon for my share in the occasion of offering trouble to your Lordshipp.*

*Your Lordshipp's* of the *4th. current* obligeth me to make this defence for myself, that as I never did so I hope I never gave your *Lordshipp* cause to think I durst expect the favour of a line from your *Lordshipp* on any other score than as your *Lordshipp* found reason to place any commands upon me, besides being conscious (in my own trade) of the different welcome I give to letters needing no answer before those that do require one. I am ambitious that mine may be of the former rather than of the latter rank with your *Lordshipp.*

23

*Wee doe lay about us all wee can to meete the Spring with a good fleete.*

*Wee are all of us amused at the ill proofe of the Royall Katherin whose lower parts are brought to but 3 foote above water before shee hath all her provisions and guns in, which (unless the lightening her of some Ballast remedy it) will prove a great disappointment as well as some reproach to us.*

*God preserve your Lordshipp*

*May it please your Lordshipp*

*Your Lordshipp's most obedient servant*

S. P.

Lord Sandwich
Jan 7th. 1664/5.

(ff. 154–5)

## LETTER XII

¶ The opening paragraph is concerned with hiring six ketches and cleaning hired ships by their own crews with materials supplied to them, on repayment, by the Navy Board. The line shaved by the binder is the only case of illegibility due to material damage in the whole volume. It appears to be a paragraph of one short sentence, the last four words of which may be as suggested. Purveyors, who are referred to more than once, seem to have been agents in the forests for selecting trees for felling. A stove was a kind of kiln into which ropes were put to make them pliable. A reference to stoving in the Diary occurs on 1664/5 Feb. 13 and there are two letters in *Further Correspondence* concerned with the building of a stove on pp. 37, 38 and 43. As to the meaning of the word 'censure', see note to letter No. 33. Blackburgh has already been mentioned in the note to letter No. 4. Sir Thomas Meres was M.P. for Lincoln and in 1679 a commissioner of the Admiralty; what his connection with the Navy Board was in 1664/5 I do not know. The unconscionable dearness of the cheap man is humour of the same type as the youngest Elder Brethren.

*Sir*

In answer to yours of this night you may please to understand that we have given thought for two *Ketches*,

24

they will be taking in their victuals to-morrow. A *third* is also agreed for and is to come up from *Sandwich*. A *fourth* we have bid money for and I believe will be taken. To-morrow morning I doubt not to have two or three more offered us, whereof two (by consent of *Sir W. Penn*) I shall endeavour to come to agreement for. I had summoned all the owners of the *merchant* ships before us this afternoon, in hopes of your company, to be treated with about the cleaning of their ships. *They* came and we after much wrangling, came to this result, that materials for their cleaning should be issued by us to their boatswains and *carpenters* to be employed by the ships' company in cleaning and *graveing* their ships. They to *reimburse* us the value of the said provision, according to the certificate which we shall produce under the hands of their said officers.

(Shaved line) .　　.　　. would bring them to(o).

The *Guinea Merchants* were also with us, to whom after long contest, we offered as much as we found *Justifiable* for us to do (the particulars whereof *Sir W. Penn* to-morrow has undertaken to tell you) and so parted, they declaring our offer unreasonable.

We have agreed with *Morehouse* to serve us as *pourveyor* in *Waltham Forest*, who shall be despatched soon as I can get the name in the warrant (which was *Lewsly*) altered by *Sir Ph. Warwick*.

I shall, as I wrote you last night, put together my informations touching *Stoving* of *shrowds*, but would not in your absence commit them to the censure of the Board and therefore forbore the mentioning the business till I can have your opinion thereon. In the meanwhile, be pleased to look over the enclosed which I had prepared for you.

However, I have adventured this night to advise *Commissioner Middleton* to look out for erecting a *Stove* in the best and speediest manner he can, and to advertise the Board what he can do thereon.

Mr. *Russell* the *pourveyor* is gone.

We have gone through with one *Merchant man* more this day (*the Blackmore*) and done in effect as much with another (the Constant *Katherine*) only their consent is respited till to-morrow morning.

*Commissioner Middleton* (to whom I have this *night* wrote about despatching the *Yarmouth* out again with masts) would know whether the *Swiftsure* should be cleaned or no. We have had *Blackbury* before us this day, but the truth is he do not give us any competent satisfaction in his case.

We have ordered *oars* to be sent presently to *Chatham*. A bill of *Imprest* is made out to Mr. *Johnson* for £1,000.

Pray be pleased to tell *Sir G. Carteret*, or by some other means, to quicken our requirements to the Lords of the *Prizes* which is this day given to them, about two or three of the *Chesnutt galliotts*, *Commissioner Middleton* in every letter minds us very passionately of the injury the King's service suffers for want of them.

*Meres's* cheap man is so *unconscionably* dear, that we cannot agree to his price for timber or plank, and have therefore this afternoon properly refused *dealing* for the parcel, and must look out for a supply elsewhere, which I *hope* will be found.

I am, *Sir*,

Your most humble servant

*Mr. Coventry*
*Feb. 9th. 1664/5.*

*S. P.*

26

# LETTER XIII (f. 156)

[Marginal note] This was writ by particular direction of Mr. *Coventry* by letter yesterday.

¶ Alice Holt was a royal forest in Hampshire. Mr Cooper has made a previous appearance in letter No. 3.

*Mr. Pett*

*The board* has pitched upon *Morehouse* for *Waltham forrest* and Mr. *Coventry* has proposed the employing one of the carpenters of His *Majesty's* ships (said to be a very able *builder* and fit for the work) to be sent to *Al*[*i*]*ce Holt*. I know you have a good respect for Mr. *Cooper* whose ability is also well known, but the terms he asks of us are very hard and such as I am confident will not be granted. Therefore I would advise you as from myself to persuade him to some easier terms and to be with us on *Tuesday* next, that if it may be, he may be entertained on that service. If you find he will not recede from his first demands, then you would do well to think of some other fit person that so you may have your satisfaction in the choice of him.

I am

Your very affectionate friend to serve you

*S. P.*

*Mr. Chr. Pett*
*Feb.* 11 1664/5.

# LETTER XIV (f. 157)

*Sir*

My last acquainted you that I had effected you another bill of imprest of £*1,000*, this is only to tell you that out of a desire to render your service to the King as free from trouble as I can to you, I will take care to call for your

27

bills of imprest up and deliver them to whom you shall appoint to receive the same, that you may be finally discharged of so much money which yet lies out as a debt upon you.

I am, Sir,

Your humble servant

S. P.

*Mr. Johnson of Yarmouth*
*Feb. 16 1664/5.*

## LETTER XV

**¶** Lord Sandwich's draught gets much attention in the Diary (1664/5 Feb. 18, 27, Mar. 2, 4, 5 and 12). It was of Portsmouth harbour, and the ablest man in town was one Burston of Ratcliffe.

*May it please your Lordshipp*

Nothing extraordinary has arisen since my last to your *Lordshipp*, nor at present appears worthy your notice. The two embassadors expected from *France* occasion very different guesses at their *errand*. The *Dutch* are for certain taking all the courses they can to be ready for us in the Spring. Besides that their *Privateers* (now in a *joynt stock*) are likely to annoy us everywhere abroad in our plantations, and ('tis said) will be suddenly out in a considerable fleet. I have this week received your *Lordshipp's Draught* and doubt not of having it done in every respect to your *Lordshipp's* liking, having put it into the hands of the ablest man in *Towne*, but it will be above a fortnight before the first will be done, the other two will be despatched in less time after. Under the words (*Described* with some *exactness*) I find some faint strokes as if your *Lordshipp's armes* were designed to stand there. Be pleased that I may

28

be informed more certainly in that. *Your Lordshipp's* family is in health and I am most glad to hear the like of your *Lordshipp's person,* which God continue.

      *May* it please your *Lordshipp*

           Your *Lordshipp's* most obedient servant

                                   *S. P.*

*Lord Sandwich*
*Feb.* 18 1664/5.

## LETTER XVI            (ff. 160–1)

¶ Sir J. Talbott's brother was Capt. Charles Talbott, at that time of the Guar(d)land according to Pepys' Register of Sea-Officers (*Catalogue of Pepysian MSS.* Vol. i, p. 411). It may come as a surprise to many that at the end of the seventeenth century there were able women contractors. Two, Mrs Russell and Mrs Bland, are mentioned in the Diary, the latter and Mrs Plea (or Pley) are mentioned in this letter. Mrs Bland is quite unknown to fame, but some interesting particulars of her being scattered about the Pepysian literature, apology need not be made for collecting them here. The following are extracts from the Diary:

"1662 Dec. 31 Above all things pleased to hear Mrs. Bland talk like a merchant in her husband's business very well, and it seems she do understand it and perform a great deal."

"1664 Sept. 8 Fain to admire the knowledge and experience of Mrs. Bland, who I think as good a merchant as her husband."

On 1664 Oct. 5 Mr Bland had left for Tangier and on 1664/5 Feb. 2 Pepys was discoursing with Mrs Bland about getting her a passage there also. This was accomplished, for she came to say good-bye on Feb. 22, which was confirmed by a final leave-taking next day. On the 27th. Pepys was both surprised and troubled to find that she had missed the ship and it cost him much trouble to find out some way to get her to the ships at Plymouth. The Diary leaves us in some doubt as to whether he succeeded, hope being all that is recorded. The paragraph in the present letter, written three days later, seems to clear up all doubt. This is the last of Mrs Bland in the Diary. She appears again in the Admiralty Journal (*Catalogue of Pepysian MSS.* Vol. iv). On p. 378 her son is mentioned as having been taken prisoner as a rebel in Virginia and on p. 417 we learn that he was executed (1677 March). On 1677 May 20 at a meeting of the Admiralty, the King being present:

"Mr. Pepys by his Majesty's particular command, communicating unto him and their Lordships a letter lately transmitted to him to that purpose by the Officers of the Navy, as having been sent to them by Mrs. Bland, mother to Giles Bland, lately executed at Virginia upon the score of the rebellion there, wherein are found words very reflective upon the Government, and the proceedings of justice against him, vindicating the innocency of her son by an irreverent comparing thereof to that of his late sacred Majesty, Was ordered to shew the same to Mr. Attorney-General, with directions to him from the King to consider and report what course is open by law to punish the author of a letter so scandalous as this must be allowed to be."

The Articles of War were the printed 'articles' that are to this day read to ships' companies. Mr Coventry had asked for them to be sent (*Cal. S. P. Dom.* 1664/5, p. 233). They are either so holy, or so difficult of comprehension, that bared heads are considered necessary while this formality is carried out.

Meres makes his second appearance (see note to letter No. 12) concerned with keel and stem pieces. Wheatley makes a laughable blunder in a note to his edition of the Diary on 1663 April 1 (*absit omen!*) where he tells his readers that 'stempieces' are 'stemples'. In some cases it may be an advantage to have stempieces naturally curved, but it is doubtful whether anything is gained by having them unnaturally twisted!

Now we come to Mrs Plea, who does not appear in the Diary at all. Her husband George Pley (this seems to be the correct spelling) was a canvas merchant who in 1660 was mayor of Weymouth, and her son was collector of customs at Lyme. On the present occasion she was able to hold her own against the Navy Board, and, from the similarity of the price, seems to have formed a 'ring' with Mr Harbin. She afterwards must have supplied Noyals (sail-cloth named after Noyal, a town in France, where manufactured) for we find Mr Pley petitioning in 1674 to recover £1350-6-0 as loss on re-drawn bills of exchange, through failure of his Majesty to pay him £70,000 owing for sail-cloth in the year 1665. Mrs Pley seems to have been the predominant partner, because in addition to conducting the negotiations in 1664, it is she who attends the Board of Admiralty in 1674/5 to hear its decision on her husband's petition, where all the satisfaction she got was:

"That a report be prepared in as much favour to his case as can consist with the doing right to the many others who may be found to have the same pretence to satisfaction for losses on the like occasion."

'Doing right' in this sense seems to mean—'Don't pay anyone, if you can't pay all'. In the *Calendar of State Papers, Domestic* for the years under consideration will be found many letters from Constance Pley to the Navy Board; they usually contain a request for some payment on account of the enormous sums owing to her. Her letters are somewhat informal in tone, and on one occasion she explains her reason for engaging in business; the letter is calendared thus:

"1665/6 Jan. 16. Constance Pley to Sam. Pepys. Sends three bills for west country commodities; can provide no more of the same quality at so low a rate, the prices being raised since the stoppage of commerce with France; will supply Noyals and Vittery canvas if any encouragement be given; business is her sole delight in this world, being formerly deprived of her children, and of late her eldest daughter was married and buried in four months; it is a charity to be kept full of employment; asks when she may expect some money for the 14 small bills sent up since September. If her offer is accepted, wishes £20,000 to be assigned her and recorded, as no money is paid but as recorded."

*Sir*

*Sir J. Talbott* having sent to me about his *Brother's* pay, I have undertaken to have a bill out for him against *Saturday*, but must be helped by you in the date of his present commission, in which his pay on the *Golden Lyon* determines. His *case* and *Capt. Seamore's* do differ from what will be the case of them that shall hereafter bring in prizes, and therefore the generality of the late resolution may perhaps be *reshaped*.

*Sir* I give you abundant thanks for your favour to Mrs. *Bland* and me on her behalf. She is gone on board *Capt. Hill*.

We have wrote this day from the Board to the *Surveyor General*, so that I hope our *purveyors* will be speedily set a-doing.

*Some articles* of *War* have been sent down to *Sir J. Mennes'* clerk in the hope however they come not to be distributed, but I have taken care thereon.

*Keele* pieces and stem pieces *Meres* says are ready.

*Junk* I have endeavoured to find. I have urged to the Board the want of it and it is committed to some persons to look out for some.

*Sir W. Warren* and Mr. *Castle* shall be here on *Saturday* to receive a *quickening* about their timbers coming in.

We have wrote to *Harwich* for a demand and the *Surveyor* says he has ordered a large supply of provisions for fitting and cleaning *Capt. Allen's* fleet to be prepared and sent thither.

*Alderman Barker's* yarn has been found bad with reason enough, but we bought it by view of *eye* of our own and therefore the merchant will think himself acquitted.

*Such* is the *outcry* made from *Chatham* for *Canvas* that Mrs. *Plea* being here we would have contracted with her for some *Noyalls* and rose to *£17-10-0 per bayle* (her last price being *£16-5-0*) but she refused unless we would give *£18*. Mr. *Harbin* also did come afterward who will not take under *£18* for what he has here, which is about 60 bales, but will have more for what he shall agree to fetch over here. We agreed with neither, the price being so unusual. Pray be pleased to think of it and as you judge fit, encourage her to bring some or not, when she comes to you for an order for a convoy, which she told us she expected suddenly from you.

No less is our want everywhere of small *masts, Chatham* having not one under 14 hands and *Deptford* wants wherewith in any degree to supply them. We have treated with Mr. *Wood* who has got all in the *river, viz.* about 300 under and 200 above 12 hands, but he declares he will not sell any but *all* (as well old as new) nor will any other price for them than a third of a penny more in every dimension than *Sir W. Warren's* price was in *July* last. Pray let me know your mind hereon, for I perceive he is very absolute in his demand.

*Col. Middleton* writes me there is a *prize* there with deals tar and some great *anchors* and other things of use for us, would you would be pleased to let it be looked after.

*Sir*

I am your most affectionate and humble servant

*Mr. Coventry*                    *S. P.*
*Mar. 2nd. 1664/5.*

The *Ipswich Maisters* of the six ships were all with us to-day and made it appear to *Sir W. Batten* and *Sir W. Penn* that for the bearing of great guns they must have all of them their decks taken up and new laid with thicker plank and better supported, with other so considerable restorations, that neither the King's service could bear with the time necessary for the doing it, nor their purses (without extraordinary advancement of money) be able to perform it, whereupon *Sir W. Penn* hoping that ships of as good force more ready might be found in the *river*, they were all for the present discharged, they and their ships.

## LETTER XVII

¶ Frank Hosier, here well spoken of, was later very much in Pepys' good books, owing to his new method of keeping Storekeepers' Accounts. At the end of October 1665 Pepys recommended him as Surveyor of Victualling at Dover. He was the father of Admiral Hosier. Sir W. Rider appears often in the Diary in varied capacities ranging from Master of Trinity House to a diarist of forty years' standing. Alderman Backwell is mentioned as often, but almost invariably in his capacity as a goldsmith.

*Sir*

*This day Capt. Taylor* has been with me to tell us of the *arrivall* of a ship of his of *New England Masts* great and small, which will be a very welcome supply to *Chatham*, whither *Sir W. Penn* and I have ordered them.

*Wee* have no answer yet from the Lords of the Council about the *Prudent Mary*, which refused our offer.

*I* have not only spoken with *Frank Hosier*, *Mr. Shelden's* clerk and find him very sensible of your favour to him, but made very particular enquiry concerning him and hear an exceeding good report of him for his sobriety and diligence. The sooner he is at *Gravesend*, the sooner the King will save money and have his work better done, I believe.

I have this day in discourse with *Sir W. Rider* found much cause to fear our *Hemp-Contract* will be trouble attended this year, he declaring, and *Alderman Backwell* too, that till they receive money they will meddle no further in it. Pray let us come to some better understanding hereon.

*Sir*

Your most humble servant

*Mr. Coventry*                                   *S. P.*
*March* 10th. 1664/5.

(f. 166)                   **LETTER XVIII**

¶ Mr Sheldon has already been mentioned in the note to letter No. 3. This letter arises out of the third paragraph of the previous one.

*Mr. Sheldon*

His *Majesty* having occasion to employ one as Clerk of the *Cheque* to attend the due mustering of ships at *Gravesend* and in the *Hope*, for the doing whereof your servant *Frank Hosier* has (out of the good opinion the Board has of his ability and diligence) been recommended to His *Royal Highness* as a person fitly qualified, His

34

*Royal Highness* has been pleased to think well of our recommendation and ordered a warrant to be provided for him accordingly. Hereof it was necessary to give you advertisement that you may the sooner provide yourself other help. His *Warrant* will be ready for him *Monday* next, so that you may then permit him to wait on *Mr. Coventry* for it. I am very glad to find such an encouragement bestowed upon him, I having always found him *carefull* in the King's and your business and shall upon the like occasions and *inducements* be always ready to befriend any related to yourself.

Remaining

*Your* very affectionate friend

*March* 11 1664/5                             *S. P.*

## LETTER XIX           (f. 167)

¶ This letter is perhaps the most interesting of the present selection, and in spite of a slightly corrupt passage at the beginning, is quite clear in its meaning. Mr Deane had submitted a design for a new ship. Although Pepys had recommended him, he is not taking any risks, so, suppressing its authorship, he shows the design to Mr Castle, who gave his opinion that the man who made the drawing had never built a ship, nor understood one. As Pett had previously spoken to Pepys of Castle himself in almost the same words, Pepys did not take Castle's judgment as final, but allowed Deane to be his own judge, returning him his drawing for revision, if necessary, with the helpful accompaniment of two rival designs, together with the dimensions of Castle's own ship, which he should work to as near as possible. Faithfulness to the King or his service is twice given as the motive for this questionable proceeding; it seems rather a case of protesting too much.

Part of what is here revealed is mentioned at a later date in the Diary, after the ship had been built:

"1666 May 19 We did then fall to discourse about his ship 'Rupert', built by him there, which succeeds so well as he hath got great honour by it, and I some by recommending him; the King, Duke, and every body saying it is the best ship that was ever built.

35

...I must confess I am much pleased in his successe in this business, and do admire [i.e. wonder] at the confidence of Castle who did undervalue the draught Deane sent up to me, that I was ashamed to owne it or him, Castle asking of me upon the first sight of it whether he that laid it down had ever built a ship or no, which made me the more doubtfull of him."

## Mr. Deane

I judge it will be some satisfaction to you to tell you that upon discourse before the *Duke* yesterday morning the *Duke* enquired who built the ship at *Harwich*. *Mr. Coventry* answered and was seconded by *Sir W. Batten* and myself that you did, with which without more discourse or question the *Duke* was satisfied, and by a letter this day from the Board you will see they [pitch] on you for the build her, whereon I wish you as good success as yourself can do.

But now I think I should not be your friend if I should not tell you what happened yesterday after*noone*. We having lately written to *Shipwrights'* Hall to appoint some person to examine all the draughts that are before us of ships to be built, which they will shortly do. I did in discourse at my house with Mr. *Castle* alone take out two draughts and desired him to look upon them, which he did, I not giving him the least notice whose they were. One he liked pretty well, which indeed is Mr. *Furzer's*, but he guesses it to be one *Monday's*. The other upon examining he finds that there is never a main breadth line marked upon it and that the frame bends do not answer the scale of the ship, nor as he says do the scale itself fit the ship. He says that the *floore* is in no degree broad enough, and to tell you the truth, did so cry out upon the lines and *proportions* as at last to swear that he that made the *draught* had never built a ship in his life, nor understood a ship.

Now I well knowing that he cannot be ignorant that *Sir W. Batten* is now become your great friend and endeavours all he can to commend you and also I from the first to the last concealing the names of the persons to whom the *draughts* belong, am much of opinion that he cannot speak this out of ill will to you, or knows that you were concerned in it.

I must confess I do wonder at it and am willing to think that he may be in an *errour* in *misjudgeing* of yours, as well as he was in the drawing of his own, for I was by when *Commissioner Pett* and my Lord *Brouncker* did examine his draught and convinced him of such gross and essential mistakes as he was forced to alter his whole draught almost, the *Commissioner* telling me alone that Mr. *Castle* had in that discovered that he knew not, nor understood, the body of a ship.

However, it being certain that Mr. *Castle* is an *artist* and has been the builder of very good ships, I could not pass by this discourse without informing you of it and that not only out of love to you, but in faithfulness to the King, and therefore, lest by haste or oversight, or both, there should be any ground for this, I will take care to send you back your draught to review, and with it the draught of Mr. *Furzer's* and another of Mr. *Shish's* of the ships they are going to build, praying you to spend some thoughts about it and to let your dimensions, as near as you can, come to what Mr. *Castle* has contracted, which is *116ft.* by the keel, *36ft.* broad, Depth in hold *15ft.*, and if you see occasion, spare not your pains to do it over again, which you may do without any reproach, none but myself knowing anything hereof, or what has passed between Mr. *Castle* and I, nor he whose draughts they were which

I did show him. This I do out of the true affection I have to you and desire of your well doing, as well as faithfulness to the King's service,

I remaining your very affectionate friend

S. P.

*March 14th.* 1664/5

LETTER XX

¶ In a letter, dated 1665 Mar. 27, Mr White acknowledges the Duke of York's warrant to act as agent for the Navy at Dover (*Cal. S. P. Dom.*).

From another letter, dated 1667 June 29, it is learnt that Mr White had been forced to terminate his employment, owing to his inability to go out of doors (*Cal. S. P. Dom.*).

*Mr. White*

Having had it long in my wishes to do you a kindness in reference to your old employment in the Navy, from the memory I have of the fair account you gave us thereof at His *Majesty's* coming in, it fell in my way yesterday to do you the good office of recommending you to the *Duke* of *York* for the same trust again, which motion of mine being seconded by the *Earle* of *Sandwich* and *Sir G. Carteret* (with whom I had discoursed before concerning it) was granted by His *Royal Highness*. Some competition there was in behalf of another, your inability to stir abroad as formerly being objected against the choosing you, but for that I undertook to satisfy His *Royal Highness* in a few days, which I intreat you be very faithful to me in informing me whether your *age* and health will suffer you to give what attendance you know the business will require, and let me hear from you by the very next post, for [if] it will, I shall with much more *assurance* prosecute what I have begun for you, and obtain His *Royal High-*

*ness' warrant* for your employment before his going to sea, which will be very speedy.

I am

Your very affectionate friend

*S. P.*

*Mr. White of Dover to bee our agent there.*
*March 14th. 1664/5*

LETTER XXI (f. 188)

*May it* please *your Lordshipp*

When your *Lordshipp* says how little I have now to say, *your Lordshipp* will not blame me for being so long silent. We are now preparing all we can (and that is but little) for the fitting ships to inforce your fleet and stores to recruit you when returned, but such is the disproportion between the charge thereof and the stock we have to do it with, that in truth (my Lord) I am very jealous one tattered fleet would puzzle us to repair it, wherefore my prayer is for peace and (which I daily repeat) for your *Lordshipp's* prosperity.

May it please your *Lordshipp*

Your *Lordshipp's* most obedient servant

*Lord Sandwich* *S. P.*
*April 8th. 1665*

LETTER XXII (f. 206)

❡ If the draughts referred to in the second paragraph are the same as those in letter No. 19, there must have been considerable delay, as the two letters are separated by seven weeks, from which it is almost safe to infer that the draughts in question are not those of Messrs Furzer and Shish.

*Mr. Deane*

I give you thanks for your last letter and the respect you appear to have had to my satisfaction in the business

39

of the lighter, The truth of it is my earnestness to have the service speedily answered at the [strait?] has I doubt occasioned my falling into a mistake about that vessel. A mistake of mine (though never so well meant) will perhaps be magnified by somebody that you know of, wherefore (as I said in my last) I desire you to let the defects of her be valued in her repairs and send me up, that I may one way or other see the King satisfied thereon, and let me know whether and how far notice thereof has or may be given to *Sir W. Batten* thereof, that I may accordingly give him satisfaction too, when he shall demand it.

You will give me notice when the *Draughts* come to your hands, that I may know that they are safe. I sent them by the man you desired a fortnight since.

Some ships will suddenly come into clean. I pray God you may be furnished with all materials and stores for their despatch and remain

Your affectionate friend

*S. P.*

Pray tell me when the other two open lighters *arrive*.
*May 4th.* 1665.


(f. 207) LETTER XXIII
*Mr. Deane*

      I kindly thank you for your last, and for the particulars of the charges laid out in fitting the close lighter which, because it is mixed with some other matters, and so not so fit to be made use of, if there should be occasion, I desire you would let me have it in a letter alone, taking notice of my desiring you to give me an account of anything wanting about the lighter, and that accordingly the charge of the caulking her (which is incident to new work) was 6 men's labour 2 days, a quarter of a barrel of pitch, about 56lb. of *oakum* and bolts drove into her (which had been forgot) weighing $\overset{\text{cwt}}{\text{o}}\overset{\text{qr}}{\text{—1}}\overset{\text{lb}}{\text{—23}}$, to which, if there be any other charge, pray add it, for I will see the King reimbursed it, whether labour or provisions.

I remain

Your very affectionate friend

S. P.

*May 6th.* 1665.

The *Duke* and Mr. *Coventry* being gone, I have forborne the sending our letter about you, but it is done as you would wish it, it being of my own doing, and then I am sure you will not doubt of its well meaning towards you.

## LETTER XXIV

(f. 208)

¶ From the tone of this letter, it is clear that when Pepys says that he believes there will be a very good correspondence (i.e. agreement) between Taylor (see note to letter No. 3) and Deane, he is fairly sure there will not be. However, he does his best to start them off well. A year later Deane has to be reproved for dishonouring of the Commissioner (i.e. Taylor), *Further Correspondence*, pp. 131, 145, while on p. 154 a reconciliation was brought about (1666 Nov. 22).

*Mr. Deane*

My present business is to tell you that *Captain Taylor* is coming down, between whom and you I do both desire and believe there will be a very good correspondence, he coming with a very good opinion of you and a respect for you. The business of the house may perhaps stick a little in his mind, and I nor you can much blame him for it, but in the first place I am resolved to see you kept where you are, yet so as to endeavour the seeing all kindness done to *Capt.*

41

*Taylor* by endeavouring for an allowance for a house for him, to which end, I would advise you to cast about for a house in the town that may be fit for him, and in everything to be very civil and respectful to him, as I know you will. Perhaps he may desire a chamber or two to lie in till he be furnished with a house, which I will prevent if I can, but if he should, I do not see any great inconvenience in it, for as to the injuring you as to your house, I would not have you fear it, for I have already told him enough as to that, that I am sure he will not attempt it. You may depend on this my advice in case he should need a chamber for the present, but I will keep him from desiring that, if any house in the town can readily be had for him. This is all from

Your truly affectionate friend

*May 9th.* 1665.                                    *S. P.*

(f. 211)                     LETTER XXV

❡ The letter in praise of Deane, written by Pepys himself, was referred to in letter No. 23, but the occasion of it is not clear. He (whom we know not) may be Commissioner Taylor, as in the previous and following letters.

*Mr. Deane*

The Duke being now returned, I have herewith sent the letter I wrote concerning your encouragement. I have sent it open, that you may read, seal and send it away when you see cause, and I doubt not but you will be satisfied with what I have said on your behalf therein, it being more than I believe was ever yet certified by this Board of any one officer in the Navy, yet nothing more than what you do very well deserve. I wish it good success on your behalf.

42

He (you know who) is coming down to *Harwich*. I have not yet had occasion to mention the smallness of the charges in the fitting of the vessel, pray endeavour to prevent any misreport or dissatisfaction in him, as much as you can, concerning it and the other two vessels also, and inform me in all that passeth, if there should be any-thing.

I am your very affectionate friend

*S. P.*

*May* 16th. 1665.

## LETTER XXVI

(f. 215)

¶ Capt. Taylor was now at Harwich and receives advice as to correspondence on doubtful things.

*Sir*

*Mr. Wood and Mr. Grey are very positive about theyr masts to sell all or none. However, some course shall bee taken to send as many as wee can, and that speedily.*

The rest of your demand also will be presently sent down.

I do much wonder how the letter came to be lost, but I will prepare another and send it you. I would advise you in matters clear and relating only to the Board, that you do write to them, and in things doubtful, or of particular concernment, write letters apart to me.

So I wish you all good success, and rest

Your truly affectionate friend and servant

*S. P.*

*Capt. Taylor at Harwich.*
*May* 20th. 1665.

43

LETTER XXVII

¶ It is sometimes remarked, with a certain amount of astonishment, that Pepys as a member of Parliament did not fulfil the promise of a career given by his two great speeches at the bar of the House, mentioned in the Diary. A possible explanation of this is that he was one of those men who are at their best only when fighting, and preferably when in defence. He seemed to have a gift for digesting and parading masses of facts and figures. The present letter is a good example of his method on a small scale. The defence is so complete, that it can be left to speak for itself.

*Sir*

You will by another from the Board this night (if you be at *Chatham*) receive to-morrow His *Royal Highness'* resolution touching the *Soveraigne*, which it is expected should be out in a very little time, and thereto your promised assistance is desired.

What I have to add is in answer to yours to me of the 12th., which I received on *Wednesday*, whereon I must own myself much surprized to find so severe a reflection upon the whole Board in the business of masts, as if they, contrary to your frequent advice, had committed some such heinous neglect in the contracting with one *man* for our supply of *Masts*, that it needed a public declaration of your incense thereon.

What I have to say is this:

1. That to this hour I never heard you, either publicly or privately, oppose this contract or offer any better or other, saving lately one with Mr. *Shorter*, which he upon treaty did voluntarily decline. This I affirm and appeal to the memory of the Board as to what you have at any time discoursed hereon at the table.

2. That at the time of the making this contract, Mr. *Wood* and others were summoned, but none would enter-

tain our supply. Mr. *Wood* declaring he would fetch no more till he had sold what he had here.

3. That no contract appearing in my books for 15 years backward (so well as things were done then) equals this in cheapness and other circumstances of advantage to the King.

4. That it was made deliberately, and by His *Royal Highness'* particular approbation, as well as full advice of the Board, and upon this one consideration, His *Royal Highness* did proceed to prefer this method of contracting at that *Juncture*, that it were fit to have some person certain to depend upon, and for the rest that might be brought to market, we were never a whit the further from buying them, besides the serving ourselves at a pinch with what were ready here, and which accordingly we have at this time bought *viz*: Mr. *Wood's parcell* of *400 masts*.

*Lastly*. I have this further to vindicate the Board with, that as you never did propose any other way so I am ready to make good, that at the time and since, no *English merchant* but *Sir W. Warren* was, and has been, able to serve us with that quantity and sort of masts as he has done upon that contract, and therefore no contrary advice of yours (if you had given any) could have been of use to us.

You will please to pardon this *unusuall* style, it being upon a matter extraordinary and in defence of the whole Board against a very *untimely* and, I think, so *unjust* a charge, as in truth I know not one thing whereon more of their care, and with better success, has at any time been exercised than this, though it answer not all our wants.

I remain, *Sir, Your* very humble servant

*S. P.*

*Commissioner Pett in answer to
his chargeing neglect in the board
in the business of masts.
June 16 1665.*

¶ According to the Diary (1664/5 Mar. 8), Batten and Mennes were of opinion that the *London*, which blew up near the Nore, could not be weighed. This letter shows that some attempt at salvage was made, but it was unsuccessful (*Cat. Pepysian MSS.* 1, p. 267). The 'mutineers', with whom Pepys was sent to take some course, were merely 'strikers'. Men in the dockyards were subject to naval discipline, being pressed when necessary (see P.S. to letter No. 46). On this occasion the strike died out; but in letter No. 37 more widespread trouble is mentioned, without any information as to the result. The Second Dutch War was carried on with very little money for the Navy; stores were obtained when possible on credit and the men were paid by ticket. The present letter gives some examples of the difficulties of the Navy Board, due to this cause. Sir Jr. Knight may be a mistake for Sir John Knight, due to confusion with Sir Jeremy Smyth. Sir John Knight was mayor and M.P. for Bristol and reported on the size of anchors made in that town in letter No. 4. It might well be that he was trying to hire a ship for the Navy at Bristol, especially as Mr Gauden, the Victualler, suggested that she should victual at Milford.

*Sir*

Capt. *Taylor* in his last gives an account of the forwardness of the fleet there sent to be heeled, and the Master Shipwright and Master Attendant desiring you might be acquainted with it, to which end enclosed is a copy thereof.

The *Black Spred Eagle* prize at *Harwich* will save us the charge of the dearer vessel I told you of on Sunday last, and is approved of by *Sir W. Batten* for a fire-ship. You will therefore be pleased to gain the Lords Commissioners' order for our having her and the *Hare*, as also two vessels here in the *River*, namely the *Coppersmith* and *White Swan*, they being named to us by the officers of the Ordnance as proper vessels to be employed in weighing of the *London*.

Be pleased to signify to the officers of the Ordnance that they hasten the removal of their stores out of the *John* and *Katherine* and *Maryland*, to prevent dead pay to the ships.

Going down by advice of the Board yesterday to take some course with the late *Mutineers* at *Woolwich*, I found *Watkins* their ringleader quietly returned to work and most of his companions. The work needing their hands, I forbore therefore to do more than put a stop on all their wages, that no tickets may be made out to them without order of this Board, which (if you judge not it enough) I have not told them the Board would be satisfied in, so that what more you think fit, shall be done.

Pray let the Commander-in-Chief at the *Nowre* be desired to direct the Gothenburg* ships back to *Harwich* soon as they are loaden.

We have fully answered Commissioner *Middleton*, saving whether the *Greyhound* when ready shall go away without convoy. The *Little Unicorne* is not there yet.

The want of money is such that (as I live) I know not what we shall do. The *Chatham* smith this day desiring that we would think of employing some other there, for that he is undone and utterly unable to go on, his whole stock and *Credit* being now in our hands. We are at a stand how to get 6 or 8 *pumps* for the fleet here, *Bradly* nor anybody being willing to trust us. *Timber* lies at *Harwich* not suffered to be brought in for want of *Money*, though *Deane* has advanced above £100 (so *Sir W. Batten* says) his part of it. *Capt. Taylor* has not money to pay the board wages of his workmen, nor the little encouragement the other day ordered to the *Carpenters* of ships which (their work being now ended) they are at him very importunately for, *et sic in infinitum etc.*

*Sir Jr. Knight* tells us he has given you an account of what he has done there, so that I need not repeat, but only

* One of the rare cases of a proper name rendered in shorthand.

*ask* would you have him entertain the small vessel of 20 guns, or stay for another?

The *Commander*, *Purser* and *Gunner* of the ship he has heard you will pitch upon and send blank warrants for him or us for the *Boatswain* and *Carpenter* to be chosen by the owners. Pray let the officers of the Ordnance be ordered to provide ammunition for what guns they shall be informed, either from *Sir J. Knight* or this office. Mr. *Gauden* desires part of the ship's victualling which is hired, may be taken in at *Millford*, where he has a great store and no employment. Let me know *Sir*, what you advise in that, I having promised him an answer against the next post.

Your most affectionate and most humble servant

*S. P.*

*Sir\* Wm. Coventry*
*June 27 1665.*
[\* 'Sir' is written over 'Mr.']

## LETTER XXIX

¶ The 'persons slain' were those killed in the fight with the Dutch off Lowestoft on 1665 June 3.

*Sir*

*You will be pleased to remember press warrants for Harwich. Commissioner Pett tells me the Soveraigne wilbe ready for victuals as fast as it can be sent (of which I have advertized the Victualler). He writ 2 days since that all the Ships are gone from Sheerness and the Zealand from Chatham; which wilbe suddenly followed by the St. George and Charles the 5th. and the Crowne also by Tuesday next.*

*I can't yet heare of a fitt mate for the Providence and which is more feared from the present scarcity of men, that without a Commander, an officer of less quallity will hardly be able in any time to man her.*

48

*I am just come from on board the Ruby, where she is in every pointe ready to saile from Deptford and hath been soe since Thursday, but the winde hath been opposite and still continues soe. The Bull is now discharged of the Ruby's stores and will soon be dispatched as Mr. Shish tells me. Truly Sir I am at a very greate loss to thinke how the Soveraigne, John and Katherine, Maryland, Ferdinand, Providence fire-ship, Deptford ketch and some Provision vessells here in the River, wilbe manned in any time, and the more from the difficulty I finde of getting Captains to doe any thing towards it, they generally leaving it to their under officers, themselves taking the care neither of getting, nor keeping of them when prest. Soe soon as I came home on Thursday morneing I fell to enquire after the Gothenburg shipps, but can't from any hand finde where the defalte is of theyr not appearing in Solebay. Capt. Taylor's money hitherto ordered is at last paid, but I feare he hath been a good while in condition to demande more, Board wages takeing upp a greate deale and indeed Sir I thinke that place hath hitherto deserved noe discouragements. Sir Wm. Warren's two New England shipps are attending convoy in the Downes which be pleased to tell me how it may be obtained.*

A Collection of Gratuitys to *Widdowes* of persons slain shall be speedily prepared for you.

Mr. *Gauden* is wrote to about the *Soveraign's* provision and Mr. *Lewes* did last night in discourse say that she should have 3 months' and that she could not receive more.

Sir,

*Your* most humble servant

*Sir W. Coventry*

*July* 15 1665.

S. P.

LETTER XXX

¶ This letter is half in longhand, which is printed in *Further Correspondence*; and half in shorthand, a photograph of which was printed in the illustrated edition of Messrs Sotheby's sale catalogue. Sir George Carteret, the addressee and Treasurer of the Navy, had a house at Cranbourne in Windsor Forest, where he was living at the time, no doubt on account of the Plague. The first part is concerned with the hire of premises for the Navy Office, which had been ordered by the King to be removed there (Diary 1665 Aug. 19).

The order is thus given in abstract:

"Aug. 15 Salisbury

"The King to the Navy Commissioners

"The great increase of infection about London and Westminster makes it inconvenient for that office, which at this time is of great concern, to continue longer there; it is therefore to be removed to such rooms in the manor house at Greenwich as shall be appointed by Sir John Denham, there to continue during pleasure" (*Cal. S. P. Dom.* 1664–5).

Certain writers over-estimate Pepys' action in staying in town, anticipating Casabianca by more than a century, with the heroic phrase 'He stood by his post when others fled'. No one with whom Pepys was associated could fairly be described as having fled; on the contrary, if anyone had to be blamed, it would have to be Pepys himself for risking his life unnecessarily in disobedience to the King's order. His death at that time, it may be imagined, would have dislocated the Navy far more than the trivial delay caused by diverting letters from Seething Lane to Greenwich. The orders consequent upon such letters at Deptford, Woolwich and Chatham could have been given more speedily from Greenwich. If then we choose to admire him for his indifference to danger, there is no reason to belittle his colleagues, or to describe them as having fled. At this time the Duke of Albemarle, better known as Monk (or Monck), was acting for the Duke of York, who had gone to York (*Life, Journals and Correspondence*, Vol. I, p. 99).

In the shorthand part of the letter, reference is made to Sandwich and Tyddiman bringing back their fleets to Solebay after the discreditable fiasco at Bergen, described in the Diary on 1665 Aug. 19. Mr Lewes was the assistant to the Victualler; this is his fourth and last appearance in these letters.

Sir

*At my leaveing you at Cranbourne I desired you to move my Lord Arlington about having the King's pleasure obtained for our hireing some rooms in a private house then offered us at Greenwich for our office. But Sir Jno. Mennes who procured the offer is since otherwise advised, and will not have the office kept at his lodging, soe we make use of His Majesty's letter, and have roomes assigned us at the King's house, where we shall meet on Satturday: But letters now comeing thick upon us from the fleet, Sir Wm. Coventry, the Duke of Albemarle and other places, requireing speedy answers and orders thereupon, I hardly see it practicable (at least for me) to be any where but heere, saveing upon the meeting daies, when I shall waite upon the rest of the officers.*

*My Lord Sandwich's Fleete and Teddimans are joyned in Solebay, and the Fresh Shipps (which were ready here) are come to them, Soe that there will bee* a noble fleet again.

*But Sir the business of the Victualling will I feare undoe us all,* if it be no better than Mr. *Lewes* himself tells me, whom I sent for and have this day run through his whole matters with him, which I shall digest to-morrow so as to give you a plain account of it by the next.

*In the meane time* I will not rest night nor day to send away what is possible to be got from hence, that (I) our fleet may be out again by times.

*Blessed* be God, our *Sound Fleete* which we had given over is well *arrived.*

*Your most humble and faithfull Servant*

*S. P.*

Sir G. Carteret
*Aug. 24th. 1665.*

# LETTER XXXI

¶ Sir Wm. Coventry's visit to Oxford was due to the Court having removed there on account of the Plague. The letter needs no explanation. The East India Ships mentioned in the postscript are the two prizes captured on September 3. See note to letter No. 34.

*Sir*

You are *ere* this, I doubt not, at *Oxford*, whence I hope to hear that you did complete your *agreement* for some *English* hemp before your coming from the *North*.

I was in hopes lately we might have been at a little leisure to look about us how to prepare matters for the next year, for I must confess myself wholly at a loss how to make a judgment of our stores *etc.* for another year's service, but by the *Duke* of *Albemarle's* letters yesterday and to-day we are to re-fit out the whole fleet presently, which (though I judge it next to impossible) shall be endeavoured with all the *vigour* we have, but you will find by the *Victualler's* accounts (which the *Duke* of *Albemarle* will send you) that he has not ready above *6 months'* dry, nor can compass so much wet provisions for *5,200* men in less than *20* days, and what that will do to a fleet of *23,000* men (for none of our mouths are yet stopped by paying off of any) you will easily compute.

You cannot be [?] to need minding in our *Money Concernments* and *Eastland Convoys*, therefore I shall forbear saying aught thereon and praying for the length of your health, rest

Your ever most humble servant

*Sir W. Coventry*                                                     *S. P.*
*Greenwich, Sept. 28th. 1665.*

My *Board* are all well, though none upon the place. *Sir J. Mennes and Lord Brouncker* being ordered to reside on board the *East India Shipps*.

LETTER XXXII (f. 241)

¶ The first part of this letter is in longhand, and is printed in *Further Correspondence*. Although there were special commissioners for the sick and wounded, of whom John Evelyn was one, the organisation seems to have failed in some way, so that much extra work was put on to the willing Pepys (see also letter No. 33). This Division of the Fleet is not the one which later caused so much trouble when, after the Dutch Invasion of the Medway, an enquiry was made into the 'miscarriages of the Navy'. The cautious Pepys, anxious for cheap hemp, is not going to be personally responsible for the payment of £10,300. By the Vice-Chamberlain is meant Sir G. Carteret, who combined that office with the Treasurership of the Navy. The present dangers that cause the writer's serious prayers are, of course, the Plague.

*Sir*

*Want of money, Numbers of Prisoners (which the Commissioners for Sicke and Wounded have flung upon us) to be fedd, of Recovered men to be disposed of, and Merchant shipps and Seamen to be paid off is the greatest of our present burthen, and is likely to bee my song to you till some thing bee done for our ease therein, which haveing soe much of the King's honour and purse concerned in it will not be left long unminded. I made a stepp* down to the fleet last *Sunday* and in my return visited *Sir W. Penn* at *Chatham*, whom I found out of order and apprehensive of being more so by his old infirmity, on which score he desires (and with much reason I believe) he may have the friendship of the shore this winter. The *Division* of the *Fleet* some to *Portsmouth*, others to the *Northward* and the rest to stay here was directed while I was there. But let me be pardoned in so often wishing for timely thought of our victualling matters against next year and securing our *Eastland* goods home, which last leads me to tell you that we are offered *200 Tons* of *Riga* and *Königsberg* hemp, now come, at *£51-10-0 per Ton* (we having lately paid *£55*,

53

and are at this day refused for less than £55 by *Capt. Cocke*) but the *Merchants* demand *£2,000 down* and *£1,000 per mensem* till it be all paid, declaring their dependence upon the persons of this office for performance of contract as to their payment. *Sir* as I know you will forward our agreeing for it, so let me entreat you for our sakes to pray the *vice-chamberlain* (to whom I have wrote about it) to make more than a temporary and general promise for the money and to signify that his undertaking to this Board, it being not a time for a man to be over free in making himself a debtor unnecessarily, though I have not at other times spared to do that for sums within my reach. *Sir* I do with all seriousness pray [for] your health during the present dangers, and am

> Your ever most faithful and humble servant
>
> *S. P.*

*Sir W. Coventry*
*Oct. 3rd. 1665.*

(ff. 242–4)                LETTER XXXIII

¶ The first two paragraphs of this lengthy letter are in longhand, the second of the two is printed in *Further Correspondence*, where, in order to complete a sentence, Dr Tanner was compelled to guess the first shorthand word. His guess of 'judgment' gives the meaning more clearly to modern readers than the actual word, which is 'censure'. In Pepys' time the word had its classical meaning of pure judgment, without any implication of adverse judgment. The paragraph in question, with its information about the documentary evidence that Pepys was keeping as to his activities in the business of the Navy, is most likely to be what he referred to when he said:

"Among the many thousands under whose observation my employment must have placed me, I challenge any man to assign one day from my first admission to this service in July 1660 to the determination of the war, August 1667,.....of which I am not this day able upon oath to give an account of the particular manner of my employing the same" (*Catalogue of Pepysian MSS.* Vol. 1, p. 33).

It is unlikely that this refers to the Diary, as has been previously assumed. In addition to desertions and want of money, plague in the yards is a new trouble for the harassed Pepys.

As to the Victualler, Pepys was much perturbed that the whole business depended on one man who might fail, betray or die, and he put forward alternative schemes, either that Mr Gauden should be compelled to have some wealthy, experienced and active partners; or that the victualling should be managed by a commission. He discussed the matter with the Duke of Albemarle by interview and letter (*Further Correspondence*, pp. 54–57). Pepys here bewails again the failure of the commissioners for sick and wounded. (See previous letter.) This reference to Mr Evelyn is the only one in these letters. Sir Philip Warwick was secretary to the Lord Treasurer.

*Sir*

> *Both yours of the 30th. of September and 3rd. current are with me.*

> *Since you were prevented, I will endeavour to have something made of your treaty about English hemp, of which provision we are in very great danger to feele a want, especially if God almighty should suffer us to neglect, or punish us with the miscarriage of our Baltique supply. My last letter of the 3rd. acquainted you with an offer of 200 tuns of Riga and Königsberg, to which I hope daily for the answer upon the point of secureing us in our personal undertaking for the paiement, which is demanded (and somewhat more particulerly from my selfe) by the Merchant.*

> *For your good advice about a timely looking after a supply of stores, I wish to God I had a better answere to give you, however lett this pass for a good one so farr as that it is the true one vzl : That I will alway so (as I have hitherto) preserve myselfe in a capacity by my Journal letter book and otherwise to proove that I have not only at all times beene mindfull to demand from the yards, but have had answerable returns from thence of the state of theire stores and what they wanted, and that I have publickly delivered these to the*

*Surveyor, and (as my duty is) minded the board of contracting or otherwise providing for supplies. But whether this will be reckoned a full acquittal of my selfe (at this time of soe much more business of my owne to do) I must submitt to my Maister's* censure, but this I will confess, I have not, nor have ever to this day, observed that anybody has made it his business to see what progress was made in the supply, or by any *forecast* calculate that and the stores to the expense by any serious and distinct comparing one to the other, nor will it (to be plain) without a miracle be ever (I fear) done by the [alone?] hands which (I take it) are charged therewith. Unless His *Royal Highness* shall be pleased by some special *act* to lay the weight of the matter upon the particular person and declare his expecting an account of any failure thereon from him singly. This is all I can say touching as well a provision of anchors as many other things as necessary, and as much wanting, and of no less difficulty to procure on a sudden as them.

For the hastening of the new ships I am fearful that what with the plague in all the yards but *Portsmouth* and *Bristoll*, and want of money (on which score *Woolwich* has already been once, and is now again likely to suffer a general desertion of the shipwrights) we may find their works [more] backward than we would have them, but I assure you no orders nor good words shall be wanting in us to quicken them, nor I hope provisions of any kind be unready for their despatch.

I have, as to the *Victualler*, in the first place got him to give me a state of our last year's declaration, out of which I have extracted what remains in each place this *5th. October* and here send it you, from whence you will see the necessity of a timely *renewall*.

Next, I have freely imparted His *Majesty's Queery* to him and received this answer. That whatever the King and *Duke* shall judge fit for him to do (be it to what inconvenience it can be to him) he will most resignedly obey, but tells me (and indeed so as I am brought to his opinion for the present) that the time necessary for the inventoring of all his goods, offices and stores with their valuation, *adjousting* of all past contracts, and infinite other circumstances, will require more time in the doing than can render the bringing in of partners practicable to him, either with respect to the King's business, or his own safety, but that which he seems to advise, is that if His *Majesty* cannot be satisfied with his single management, that it may be managed by a Commission, as it was in the last *Dutch Warr*, upon account, which Commission to begin with the next declaration, and himself after perfecting of the last to be concerned in the next, or left out with such consideration for the use of his houses and remains of *Stocke* as to His *Majesty* and His *Royal Highness* shall seem fit.

His *Grace* the *Duke* of *Albemarle* was pleased to send for me this morning about this business and shewed me your letter. I acquainted his Grace with what I have here wrote, who at first hearing took some satisfaction in this proposal of a *Commission* and commanded me against tomorrow to think of, and name to him, some man that may *occurr* to me fit to propose to His *Royal Highness*, himself naming *Sir W. Rider*.

But as it will require a great deal more deliberation to determine concerning the way of settling this, so if a commission should be found the best, I am at a very great loss for my part where (if it were for my thought) to choose 4 men of experience *joyned* with integrity, diligence and *activity* adequate to this service and could wish I could say that I were in all of them satisfied with the fitness of the person already named, though he is not like to be bettered by many that I can think of. You may please to be thinking of this till the next post brings you more.

I am all alone, therefore cannot yet answer you about the *Harp*.

It is an unspeakable vexation that the business of the prisoners and sick and wounded brings upon me, through the failure of the commissioners proper for that charge, it costing me more *clamourous* petitions to answer, letters, orders and grants, to see so much hardship put upon poor creatures (as it this day is offered to them) than half all my other business, and is not to be removed but by some things out of my reach. Pray see what Mr. *Evelyn* has wrote me to-night since my being with him an hour before about this matter.

As to your commands touching the giving you some light into the reason of the excess of charge in this year's service and an estimate of what the charge is, I must beg you to allow me a day or two time to do it, and both to yourself and to *Sir Ph. Warwicke* (by am I whom by no means be* thought forgetful of what he lays on me) I desire to be excused for my present unreadiness having something (you will allow me) always to do, and not the assistance of any one hand a fortnight together these three months, but I will not fail to prepare what I can for you, to be with you before the *Parliament* meets.

I have summoned the *slop-sellers* and shall tell you shortly what they say in their matters, but want of money will be the burden.

* (by whom I would by no means be etc.)

I must also refer you to my next for answer to your Queery about the method of paying sick men on shore, and with tenders of most affectionate wishes for your happiness, remain

Your most humble and faithful servant

*Sir W. Coventry*                                    *S. P.*
*Oct. 5th. 1665.*

## LETTER XXXIV

¶ The first paragraph shows yet once more the state of the Navy owing to want of money. The second paragraph, as well as letters Nos. 35 and 39, together with the last paragraph of No. 37 refer to the Prize-Goods Scandal, which is mentioned on not less than eighty-one days in the Diary between 1665 Sept. 10 and 1669 May 28. There is a letter on this subject in *Further Correspondence* on p. 192, and an interesting supplementary account of it by Pepys himself in Smith's *Life, Journals and Correspondence of Samuel Pepys Esq. F.R.S.* Vol. 1, pp. 104–108, where one learns with much astonishment that W. Hewer was in a position to lend Pepys £500 to pay Cuttance and Pierce for some of the goods. This is manifestly improbable on the face of it, and it is not in agreement with the corresponding entry in the Diary (1665 Sept. 18):

"After dinner Cocke did pray me to help him to £500 of W. How, who is deputy Treasurer, wherein my Lord Brouncker and I am to be concerned and I did aske it my Lord, and he did consent to have us furnished with £500 and I did get it paid to Sir Roger Cuttance and Mr. Pierce etc."

Mr O. E. Holloway of the Bodleian Library has kindly inspected the original manuscript, and reports that the name is clearly W. How.

For convenience of reading, without referring to other books, the following brief summary of the Prize-Goods Scandal is given:

During the operations after Bergen on 1665 Sept. 3, Sandwich captured two East India ships, the Golden Phœnix and Slothany, which were very rich prizes. The correct procedure was, of course, to bring them in and hand them over to the Commissioners for Prizes and have them condemned as prizes in a properly constituted court, after which the value would be distributed to those entitled to share. Sandwich apparently knew what this meant, so he devised a simplified procedure, which he thus described to Pepys (Diary 1665 Sept. 23):

"My Lord telling me that he hath taken into his hands 2 or £3,000 value of them: it being a good way, he says, to get money, and afterwards to get the King's allowance thereof, it being easier, he observes, to keepe money when got of the King than to get it when it is too late.'

Pepys bought some of the goods in partnership with Capt. Cocke whom he endeavoured to use as a cat's paw and for a time succeeded, but the matter leaked out and the goods were seized and in spite of Sandwich's getting the King's pardon, his enemies were so strong against him, that he was given the merciful oblivion of an ambassadorship in Spain. Pepys managed to keep in the background until the end of 1667, when the outcry against the Navy Board, owing to the Dutch Invasion of the Medway, was so great that a committee of enquiry was appointed and an informer told the House of Commons 'that he did see one of the Commissioners of the Navy bring in three waggon-loads of prize-goods into Greenwich one night'. The enquiry was still going on at the end of the Diary, but no great harm came to Pepys, nor to Sandwich, for he was afterwards in a command at the Battle of Solebay, where he lost his life in 1672. Some documents having an important bearing on this matter are mentioned in the *Calendar of State Papers, Domestic*, 1665–6, pp. 218, 278 and 279.

The present letter, the longhand counterpart of which is in the *Sandwich MSS.*, shows the faithful Pepys warning Sandwich of the first sinister happenings, arising out of the disposal of the prize-goods.

*May it please your Lordshipp*

The business of the *Dutch* coming upon our coast has given us a great alarm and put us upon endeavouring to make up a fleet for them, and what is more the *Duke* of *Albemarle* had resolved to embark himself this morning, and commanded me (which I had done) to get a *Yacht* ready to carry him to the fleet, but on a sudden I have orders to forbear further endeavours, and I think for my part in a very good hour, for I am confident it had been but to have discovered too much of our nakedness, for after all, a fleet could not have been got out, nor kept out.

I have been in very great pain, and still am, on your *Lordshipp's* behalf, touching the business of these prize-goods, very severe orders being issued for the seizing on all men's, nay accordingly even those for which your *Lordshipp's Certificates* and the *Customehouse Entrys* for the payment of the *Dutys* are shown, and among them all *Capt. Cock's*. And further, my Lord *Brouncker* has wrote me word that the King and the *Duke* do disown their order or allowance in the *case*. Whence this arises, your *Lordshipp* can best tell upon the place, but I pray God there be no *foule* meaning towards your *Lordshipp* in it, for if it had arisen barely from a general *caution* against *embezzlements*, they would certainly have excepted such goods as had been disposed of with the privity and by order of your *Lordshipp*. This *ill* consequence it has, that it sets all men's tongues a-going upon the small proceed of all our *prizes*, and that it had been better they had been sunk, than for their sakes and their plunder the whole fleet should be brought in, and leave the *Dutch Masters* of the sea. Your *Lordshipp* knows, I understand, better the necessity of the fleet's coming in, but 'tis fit you should know what the World *babbles*, and compare it with the *usage* you find touching the poor kindness you have offered to yourself out of so great a prize. If I *overvalue* this *ill-dealing* your *Lordshipp* meets with, or am mistaken in it, I beseech your *Lordshipp* correct me, for I must confess myself very apprehensive of the ill use which is, or may be, made of this *Act* of your *Lordshipp*.

God preserve your *Lordshipp's* health and every other content to you, is the prayer of

Your *Lordshipp's* ever obedient servant

*S. P.*

*Lord Sandwich*
*Greenwich October 10th. 1665.*

LETTER XXXV

¶ This letter is undated, but it bears internal evidence of its date, as Pepys says 'I made it my business to go to Erith this day'. According to the Diary he went there on Oct. 11, but the longhand transcript of this letter in the possession of the present Earl of Sandwich is dated Oct. 12.

The 'certain person' to whom Sir Christopher Myngs made his remarks about Sandwich, was Capt. Cocke, as may be seen from the parallel passage in the Diary on 1665 Oct. 10.

*My Lord*

What I did acquaint your *Lordshipp* with my fear of in my last of the 10th., I am now too much confirmed in by a multiplied seizure made upon *Capt. Cocke's* goods. One by the Farmers of the *Customes*, another by a warrant from the *Duke* of *Albemarle*, and a third by *Mr. Seamour* in behalf of the *Commissioners* for *Prizes*. I did cause myself to be at the *Duke's* while *Capt. Cocke* came to his Grace's, where the *Duke* did speak with civil regard to your *Lordshipp's* warrant, but notwithstanding urged the King's warrant for the seizure, only was contented that upon security the goods should be put into *Capt. Cocke's* possession, which however through some new difficulties is not yet done. I made it my business to go to *Erith* this day, where I find my Lord *Brouncker* and *Sir Jo. Mennes* by a very strict command from *Court* busy in taking [depositions of] the manner, persons and times taken in the breaking of *Bulke*, which I find are very particular touching (among others) *Sir W. Berkeley*, but yet that your *Lordshipp's* order was produced for their doing it and that it was said by some at the doing it, that it was no matter, your *Lordshipp's* back was broad enough to bear it. It is said, and I believe it is true, that *Sir G. Askue* is one of the great *Malcontents*, for he has declared that he did from the beginning oppose the taking out of any goods, and resolves not to receive any of them otherwise than to deliver them to the King's officers, and that *Sir W. Penn* and he upon this score are at *odds*. *Sir Ch. Mings*, I hear, is another, which I the rather believe for that at his late being here in his way from *Oxford*, he did to a certain person much enlarge upon the disrespects he had received from your *Lordshipp*, instancing in his waiting three or four hours together at *that Earle's* (so he phrased it) *Cabbin* door for *audience*, and at last failed of admittance.

In *fine 20 Commissions* I believe there are out for the finding out of these goods in whosesoever hands, with very bitter *aggravations* of the *act* of selling them, and from none more *furiously* than from *Mr. Seamour* to myself and *Capt. Cocke* on board my Lord *Brouncker*, notwithstanding his false compliment he sends your *Lordshipp* this day in *Capt. Cocke's* letter enclosed.

Your *Lordshipp owes* very much to the civility of my Lord *Brouncker* in this business, who has been very tender of your *Lordshipp's honour* and made others less rude in their proceedings than they would have been, and more, he showed me a letter from his *Brother* (in your absence from *Oxford*) expressing the same regard to your *Lordshipp* in moving the *Duke* (and the King also) for the suspending the execution of their orders for *Seizure*, but with bad success from the *Duke* and a very severe denial from the King.

Not having any instructions from your *Lordshipp* how to behave myself, I dare not adventure to say or do anything in this business, saving making my observations of what others say and do. Wherefore I do humbly beg your *Lordshipp's* direction herein, and nothing shall be left undone that your *Lordshipp* shall command me, for I must assure your *Lordshipp* nothing in all my life ever went so near my heart, as the apprehensions of the *dishonour* threatened to your *Lordshipp* by several that I have understood are concerned in the *Inquisition* now on foot, and one thing I perceive already done, which is, that the *Customehouse* entries are already taken and the value of the goods disposed of must by that means unavoidably appear and what every man's share amounted to. I heartily pray for your *Lordshipp's* content and particularly in the issue of this business, and rest

Your Lordshipp's most obedient servant

*Lord Sandwich*                              [No signature or initials]

LETTER XXXVI

¶ For some reason, perhaps the one stated, Pepys seems unwilling to name his Surveyors and Surveyor-General until the salaries are settled. The reason given sounds unconvincing and it is hoped that it is not uncharitable to suggest that the real reason was that he himself was not going to be Surveyor-General unless it were worth his while, for he says quite bluntly in letter No. 38 that he has an eye to the reward and would be glad to get more honestly. 'Painful' persons are, of course, 'painstaking' persons.

*May it please your Grace*

In obedience to your Grace's letter, wherein you are pleased to acquaint me with His *Majesty's* and His *Royal Highness'* and your Grace's approbation of what I had humbly proposed, touching the settlement of the victualling, and command me to consider of the means of putting the same in speedy execution, and particularly to name to your Grace persons fit to be imployed thereon. I have

not neglected to lay together such particulars as may hereafter lead me to the presenting your Grace with instructions fit to be given to these persons when *authorized* to
receive the same and in the mean time do humbly advise
that His *Majesty* and His *Royal Highness'* pleasure may be
known what allowance shall be established before the
persons be proposed for the preventing the upbringing of
the salary to the person when named, rather than to his
work, and thereon in obedience to your command I do take
the boldness to propose that he which shall perform the
Office of *Surveyor* of a victualling port faithfully, according to the instructions which shall be presented shortly
to your Grace, will very well deserve *per annum* as
followeth

|  | £ |
|---|---|
| *Dover* | 100 |
| *Plymouth* | 100 |
| *Yarmouth* | 100 |
| *Harwich* | 150 |
| *Portsmouth* | 150 |
| *London* | 200 |

And he that shall receive the weekly ⎫
accounts from all these and keep a ⎟
constant and general check over the ⎬ 300
whole victualling action ⎭

1100

This £1100 if bestowed on persons painful and prepared
with clerkship proper for this work will, I question not,
both answer all the ends intended in my late proposal to
the prevention of the inconvenience therein mentioned
and repay itself to the King both times over in what it shall

save His Majesty out of some practices of pursers, which the instructions of these *Surveyors* shall *obviate* if well observed. The sooner His *Majesty's* will is declared herein, the sooner the business will be settled, and every day's delay is now considerable. It would also be speedily known whose care it shall be to take the engagement of Mr. *Gauden's* two sons as was proposed, your Grace having said nothing to me in your letter touching that particular.

I have discoursed with the *Victualler* about his provision of cask for the next year, and he do declare that the service cannot possibly be supported with that commodity but from Hamburg, where he has (so he says) 8,000 tuns ready. I beseech your Grace let not the difficulty be hazarded which is well remembered had like to have over-*thrown* our whole success the last *Dutch* war, and would have come very near it this year, had we had drink to have tried it.

        My Lord

                Your Grace's most obedient Servant

                              *S. P.*

*The Duke of Albemarle*
*Oct. 14th. 1665.*

                LETTER XXXVII

¶ The 'Parliament's bounty' is described in the Diary on 1665 Oct. 15 as: "The Parliament, it seems, have voted the King £1,250,000 at £50,000 per month, tax for the war".

The hemp contract is, with little doubt, that referred to in letter No. 32, where Pepys told Coventry that he had written to Carteret about it, and especially about himself being personally relieved from being made liable for the payment. Mr Kingdon was a Prize Officer and Col. Reames (or Rheymes) a Commissioner for Sick and Wounded and Prisoners of War. (See Evelyn's Diary for 1664 Oct. 27 and 1672 June 2.) The strike in the three yards is a further consequence of the moneyless state of the Navy. It is to be regretted that it is not known what Sir R. Ford's usage of Pepys was on this occasion. On the other hand, one of his two 'villainous knaveries' is known, for Pepys records on 1662 June 4, after testing Sir R. Ford's Holland's yarn and finding it to be very bad, that 'some of it had old stuff that had been tarred, covered over with new hemp, which is such a cheat as hath not been heard of'. Sir R. Ford was a Sheriff, and it is presumably in this capacity that he got even with Pepys, by getting him rated more heavily than Sir Wm. Batten.

The confession that Pepys was a partner of Cocke in the prize-goods business has the ulterior motive of being preparatory to the request that Carteret would get Cocke relieved from giving a bond for the goods.

Carteret was naturally on Sandwich's side, his son having married Lady Jemimah Mountagu on 1665 July 31.

*Sir*

I have much reason to give you thanks for your last letter, first for your good news of the *Parliament's* bounty which God send well paid and well husbanded, next for your furtherance in the hemp contract, wherewith the *Merchants* are well satisfied and we shall have the goods in our stores the next week, then for your kindness to the sick and wounded, though I do not hear by Mr. *Kingdon* that he is in cash to pay it so soon as it should be. I have delivered the warrants to Mr. S—— and *Col. Reames'* bill also. For the men that are so troublesome to the office, I do not think there have been so few as 200 here all this day ready to starve and nowhere to go, the *Captains* most barbarously refusing to receive them on board or give them tickets, by which means several die daily in the very streets and highways, as I myself am to my grief a witness.

One thing further there is, which I wish to God could be remedied, the yard at *Deptford* and the yards at *Wool-wich*, both dock and rope yards, revolted yesterday wholly from their working, declaring they would work no longer without money, so that there is at this time not a wheel nor a hammer going in all three yards, but of the officers and their servants. I am here left alone with so much of the office business to do, that I cannot go among them to see what I can do by fair or foul means to remedy this, however I am labouring by private instructions to bring them in of their own accord, if I can, on Monday (though I much despair of it) for I cannot tell how else to do, till I hear from you. Be pleased to let me have your direction about it soon as you can, for I have not taken any notice hereof to *Sir W. Coventry* in my letter, nor will till you think fit.

I have thanks to give you for your kind opinion of my letter about the victualling and do hope, if God sends us another year's war, that *action* shall be managed with much more satisfaction than it has been this, if proper persons be pitched on for *Surveyors* of the *Ports*, and the instructions be observed which shall shortly be presented to you for your allowance or amendment.

Lastly I have not thankfulness enough to give you for your kind resentment of *Sir R. Ford's* usage of me, who poor man has on me a long revenge for my detecting him in a couple of villainous knaveries about four years since, but I was in good hopes he had done with me when he got me rated at £*36* for my office of £*350 per annum* and helped *Sir W. Batten* for £*24* for his office of £*490 per annum*.

I must confess I was and am a partner with *Capt. Cocke*, though for some convenience to us both, I have rather endeavoured to be thought unconcerned therein, but God knows what we did was with as much plainness and openness, as if we had bought goods upon the *Exchange*, and thought it for my part as lawful, things appearing to us as they did, but much trouble we had made with and with much disrespect to my Lord from them, that I could not have expected it, however this night *Cocke* hopes to have some of them in possession upon bond given for his being accountable for them to the *Lords Commissioners* of Prizes. Now *Sir* that which he and I desire (if it might be) is that by some order he might be excused from giving this bond, or that the bond (if given before your advice comes) may be delivered up to him again, for while he holds them but as an accountant unto others for them, he cannot judge himself in safe possession of them, nor know how to make any honest or profitable disposal of them. Be pleased to communicate this with my most humble duty to my Lord, to whom I have given twice this week an account of what has *occurred* to me touching this business. The town, I hear, talks as if *Sir Chr. Mings* had been doing ill offices at *Court* about my Lord, pray let me know the truth of it. *Sir* I pray God continue happiness to both your families, and remain

Your ever faithful and humble servant

S. P.

*Sir G. Carteret*
*October 14th. 1665.*

## LETTER XXXVIII

(ff. 263–4)

❡ More than half this letter is in longhand and has been printed in *Further Correspondence.*

The Chatham Chest had been founded by Drake and Hawkins in 1588 to provide pensions for disabled seamen, the funds being derived from money stopped out of the seamen's pay. The letter describes in some detail one of the abuses it was subject to.

Although this letter is dated five days later than No. 36, the time still seems unripe for the Surveyors to be named. The longhand part hints very strongly at the one and only person for Surveyor-General and from the shorthand part we learn that 'the first letter of this man's name is S. Pepys', which is an unusually complete initial. The modesty and tact of the rest of the letter are noteworthy.

*Sir*

*In answer to yours of the 17th. I will not faile to write againe to the Commissioners for Sick and wounded about theire bookes against we have any paies.*

*You shall speedily have an accompt of all I can informe you touching widdows and orphans. And for what Mr. Prin hints about the chest, It is soe farr the present practice, that the mony due from each man to the chest is sett in a Columne by itselfe ready at any time to be cast up, but generally is not totalled till the tickets of all men in the booke be brought in, which is usualy a great while after the shipp be paid. But Sir that which is a thing much to be lamented is that the mony actually paid by me at my discharge to-day shall not perhaps be made good to the chest in 12 months after, nay by a late address from the Governours they declare that at this time of want among the old, and encreas of the number of new pentioners they have not received one penny of all the mony which hath been stopt from the chest since December 1663. Therefore it were indeed an act worthy his Royal Highness to enjoyne us strictly that the mony defalked at all paies be actually at the same time layd by for, or paid into some body's hand for the use of the chest, which I am glad of this occasion to recommend to you to promote, it being a thing I have frequently had in my wishes, and now see, and heare, the want of it more than ever.*

*The obtaining of what more masts are to be had in Sweden I doe judge of mighty moment, and will propound it to my fellows as soone as I can.*

*This evening I was sent for by his Grace the Duke of Albemarle, principally about the dispatching the Victualler's business and the nameing of persons fitt for the emploiement of Surveyors, which I desired a little time to doe, being very*

*unwilling to make an over suddaine nomination, though I must*
*confess I have not neglected all this while to be casting about*
*by what hands it may be well performed, and to be sure*
*cannot scape him whome you meane in your letter to the Duke,*
*But as the rendring theire service usefull will principally*
*depend upon his dilligence and care, that hath the putting*
*together, and reporting what rises from the several informa-*
*tions from every port, Soe I am at the greatest loss whom to*
*pitch upon for the emploiement.*

*The truth is I know one, that if you shall thinke fitt to have*
*it propounded to I dare go farr in assuring you the worke*
*shalbe done to your minde, for I am sure he will take paines at*
*it, and stay by it, and (which is more) will by his other*
*occasions be ever at hand, both for the ready receiving as well*
*as giving directions, and answers in all matters relating to this*
*business.*

*His emploiement in another capacity I confess is very full,*
*but halfe the trouble which this will adde wilbe saved by the*
*ease it will bring him in the many letters, orders, messages,*
*and mental labours he now is exercised with,* for want of an
easy and thorough understanding of the *victualling* action,
and the first letter of this man's name is *S. Pepys.*

And now *Sir* as I cannot say but I have an *eye* to the
reward, and would be glad honestly to get more than I
do by encreasing my pains, while God Almighty gives me
health to do it, so if I could have thought on one for
whose resolutions of performing the work I here so fully
have undertaken, upon my word I would have forborne
my own name and shall for all this most resignedly ac-
quiesce in what you shall say to it, for I am sure if you
judge it to the King's purpose, you will favour that part
which respects my accommodation, and if you think it

otherwise, I beg by no means you should scruple telling me so.

Be pleased only to give me your advice soon as may be that some body else may be timely thought on in case you think it best, or if you shall (whereon pray be very indifferent) [approve?] of my offer, I could rather desire you would please to be the mover of it than be put to solicit in a case wherein I may be thought more concerned than I am. I shall only add that I shall be able to spare a very good encouragement to an able clerk, whereby this business shall bring me a much less addition of *Worke* than it threatens at first hearing, and will indeed cost any man else but myself.

>  *I am Sir*
>
>> Your most humble and most affectionate servant
>>
>>> *S. P.*

*Sir W. Coventry*
*Greenwich, Oct. 19th. 1665.*

(f. 308)

# LETTER XXXIX

❡ The longhand counterpart of this letter is preserved in the *Sandwich MSS*. It has been printed in the *Occasional Papers* of the Pepys Club with two slight inaccuracies: the date is given as Nov. 22 and 'receiving' in line 22 is printed 'recerving'.

W. Howe was Deputy Treasurer of Sandwich's fleet. (See note to letter No. 34.) He had got himself into trouble by some dealings in precious stones. The first information was given by Madam Williams (Lord Brouncker's mistress) who referred to eight bags of precious stones. W. Howe got 'clapped by the heels' and on investigation the matter appears to have been very trivial, for Pepys contemptuously says 'we opened the chests and saw the poor sorry rubys which have caused all this ado'.

Seeing the extent to which Capt. Cocke was interested in the matter, his valuation of the prize cargoes may not have been so reliable as Pepys suggests. For previous references to the Prize-Goods Scandal see letters Nos. 34 and 35.

*My Lord*

In obedience to your *Lordshipp's* of the *23rd*. I shall look after the business of *W. Howe* and give you the clearest and speediest account I can of it.

The *Duke* of *Albemarle* is coming to *Oxford* and sets out I hear on *Tuesday* next.

I judge it not impertinent to tell your *Lordshipp* that upon late discoursing with him about the proceed of these two prizes, which I told him I believed would be between 2 and *300,000£*, I remember he replied that the embezzlement must needs have been great, for that their *Cargos* cost £*400,000* in *India*. I have since reflected upon this and judging it a fresh way of diminishing what is due to your *Lordshipp* from what these ships at this necessitous time do really produce, by magnifying what they first cost in *India*. I have made enquiry what the value of the ships is reckoned to have been in *India* and do find, and by such authority as your *Lordshipp* if necessary may make use of it, that the *Cargos* of all 13 ships cost not above £*350,000*, at most under £*400,000*, this *Capt. Cocke* assures me.

Your *Lordshipp's* money shall be ready at a day's warning, but though I can without, yet it would be convenient to have the *vice-chamberlain's* consent to my paying *Capt. Cocke's* bill out of the money I am receiving for the office. I desire your *Lordshipp* to move the *vice-chamberlain* in his next letter to give me a word or two to that purpose. The bill is £*948*.

My Lord

Your *Lordshipp's* most obedient servant

S. P.

I have wrote myself to the *Vice-Chamberlain* about *Capt. Cocke's* bill.

*Lord Sandwich*
*Nov.* 25 1665

73

¶ The 'new Act' was the vote for £1,250,000 mentioned in the note to letter No. 37. The idea seems to have been at first that the goldsmiths would be willing to advance money on the strength of this vote, but they showed themselves most unwilling. (Diary 1665 Nov. 27.) Failing this, the next thing was to attempt to get goods supplied on credit and Sir George Downing (Pepys' former master) informed Pepys that no one could induce people to serve in goods and lend money on the Act, better than he. (Dec. 12.) On the 16th Sir G. Downing was overjoyed that Norway and other goods to the value of £3650 had been obtained. (Diary and letter on p. 89 of *Further Correspondence*.) Downing showed his joy by suggesting that Pepys should lend £200 upon the Act, but he desired to be excused.

*Sir*

I gave you in my last an account how I have been pressed by *Sir G. Downing* and have since been, by a particular command from His *Royal Highness* by *Sir W. Coventry*, directed to use my utmost industry to procure credit for money or goods on the new *Act*. I told you also then that I was in expectation to prevail with *Sir W. Warren*, and have this morning at the Board agreed with him for a ship's loading of *Norway* goods to £2,000 value and about 5 tons of *Königsberg* hemp, valued about £250, to be served in immediately on the fund of the *Act*, and another ship's loading at *Harwich* newly arrived of about £1,400 value of *Norway* goods.

This I hope will convince the World that you nor I do not oppose the *Act*, for I tell *Sir G. Downing* I have been directed by you as well as by *Sir W. Coventry* to promote it, and he tells me (which I would be glad to know the truth of) that you yourself advance £1,000 upon it, which if you do I think is a very prudent act, though a great deal more than this will not serve out the next year's fleet, nor pay the wages of this.

I long to hear how my noble Lord and yourself do, you having been silent both a great while.

*Sir*

Your most humble servant

Sir G. Carteret                             S. P.
Dec. 16 1665.

## LETTER XLI            (f. 332)

¶ The fears for the safety of the ships arose presumably from the season of the year. Mr Wren was later Sir Wm. Coventry's successor as secretary to the Duke of York.

*Sir*

*I have not yet had it in my way to take the advice of any able Master touching the sending for the remainder of our Masts this yeare. But Sir W. Warren I have spoken who* says that nothing can be more advisable than to send ships away soon as these are unloaded, or sooner if they can be had, and undertakes that whereas he has 15 ships loaden there ready to ship, he will cause them all to [be un-?] loaden in 16 working days at most, and by what he knows of the trade, judges they may with safety enough go by the time such a number of ships will be got ready, which must be the latter end of *January*, and if so, they may be back before (so he judges) the [?] can be expected abroad.

I have written to all the yards to hasten them in the discharging these ships all that may be, and will by my next tell you what the seamen say to it.

I shall not till then have enough at the Board to give you their opinion about *Master Attendants*.

What I did the last post as directed by the Board, I now [do] by the particular desire of my Lord *Brouncker*, in enclosing two or three proposals of his more, touching

75

our money matters and pray your pardon that your trouble comes to you through my hands.

*Capt. Harly*(?) shall have a letter from us speedily and so shall one *Mr. Fincham*, a *Norfolk gentleman* who has made us a tender of serving the King with *English Hemp*. He has been invited to it by Mr. *Wren*, for which please to thank him when you meet.

I have again now spoken with *Capt. Cocke* who concurs in the safety as well as expediency of sending for our masts this year.

> *Sir*

> Your most humble and most affectionate servant

> *S. P.*

*Sir W. Coventry*
*Dec. 26th. 1665.*

LETTER XLII

¶ Pepys seems to fear that Sir George Carteret (the Vice-Chamberlain) misunderstands his attitude to the Act referred to in letter No. 40.

*May it please your Lordshipp*

My Lord I have some reason to suspect the *vice-chamberlain* mistakes the intent of my endeavours to promote the credit of the late *Act*, though he knows it is as himself advised me at the begin[ning], when I desired his direction thereon, and besides I have not only in every letter been pressed thereto by *Sir W. Coventry*, but by the *Duke* of *York's* command particularly directed to myself, and do lie under the observation of the *Duke* of *Albemarle* and *Sir G. Downing* how I behave myself therein, and I am sure should I not be thought a friend to the *Act*, it

76

would quickly be objected to *Sir George* as a *crime*, as well as to myself. I am not ignorant that the good success of the *Act* would be of personal detriment to him, but I know also that it is not my assistance that will make it so successful, if it had not an intrinsic worth of its own to gather credit from, and that I dare pronounce it has not, to the degree as to serve the present occasions of the Navy. Therefore pray my Lord clear him in his apprehensions concerning me, for his concernments are become *your Lordshipp's* and therefore I must and will be faithful to him.

> I humbly take leave, may it please your
> *Lordshipp*
> Your *Lordshipp's* most obedient servant
> *S. P.*

*Lord Sandwich*
*London Jan. 9th. 1665/6.*

## LETTER XLIII  (f. 361)

¶ The story about Lord Craven is also given in the Diary on 1665/6 Jan. 7, where the informant is given as Capt. Cocke. Writing six days later, Pepys says 'at dinner where I was this day'.

*Sir*

> *my last gave you an account of my procedings in receipt of the £3,000 you expected from the Custome(r)s.*

> *I allsoe told you I should procure a letter from the Board touching what they judge will bee the issue of the new Act as to a Supply of Stores therefrom, which they are desireous to take a little more time for, least they bee found over forward in theyr report; but as to any hopes of having any helpe in Mony from it, they have in a letter this day to Sir Wm.*

77

*Coventry among other things wrott as the enclosed will informe you.*

I thought it becoming me to inform you that at dinner where I was this day, one did very confidently report of his own knowledge (and he is very nearly related to him) that my Lord *Craven* is looking after the *Treasurer*ship of the Navy and reckons himself assure of it, though it be a thing I in no degree can imagine, yet believing it may not be unuseful for you to know what is discoursed of this kind, I think it requisite to tell it you.

I am *Sir*,

Your most faithful and humble servant

*Sir G. Carteret.*                                            *S. P.*
*Jan.* 13  1665/6.

¶ The business of Pursers occupied Pepys' thoughts very considerably just before this and the result was the well-known New Year's Gift to Sir Wm. Coventry, which is printed in *Further Correspondence*, pp. 93–111. As it covers eighteen and a half pages, readers interested must be satisfied with the reference.

The third paragraph seems to refer to some proposal for paying taxes in kind.

*Sir*

*myne of the 16th. has answered yours of the same date about the reception my paper of the Pursers-matters found with the Board.*

I enclose you an estimate of what the ships at *Chatham* will come in money to satisfy to the *1st. August* for the number of men on board, without tickets for men discharged.

I have also enclosed you Mr. *Gauden's* answer to a proposition made by the Lord *Treasurer* to the gentry of *Yorkshire* touching paying the *Assessment* money in provisions.

*Sir Jer. Smith* shall be speedily written to.

I meant whether the Prize Officers at *Hull* might be prevailed with (as the Farmers of the *Customes* do) to furnish us with money abroad, and trust to *Sir G. Carteret's* satisfying them here.

I rest

Honoured *Sir*

Your most humble and faithful servant

*Sir W. Coventry*                    **S. P.**
*Jan.* 18 1665/6.


LETTER XLV                    (f. 382)

¶ 'My Lord Generall' was an earlier title of the Duke of Albemarle. The waste of cask and beer was due to the very limited stowage capacity in the ships of the period. Much had to be stowed between decks and if the working of the guns were hindered, it would be thrown overboard. The *Swiftsure* had been missing since The Four Days' Fight with the Dutch, 1666 June 1–4. The rumour here recorded was unfortunately not true, as she was captured by the Dutch on the first day.

*Sir*

 *His Royall highness was pleased last night to give me severall Letters, from your selfe, Sir Wm. Penn and one from my Lord Generall, commanding me to gather out of all what workes were to be done for the dispatching of the fleete out againe. I did it and attended him with the board this morneing, where (as you devise) every person had his share*

79

*cut out for him, and I hope you will have a speedy accompt of our doeing as much therein* as our present state will bear. I assure I will not be in arrear in mine, if my promised pains night and day will do it.

I shall send you to-morrow what you may expect as to lighters and the despatch of the merchant ships down the river.

If, as it is said, the waste of cask and beer has been great during this engagement for making of room, we shall be liable to a great mis-reckoning unless some present account could be taken of the present state of the fleet as to beer, what it ought to be I can well tell according to a regular consumption since their entry into sea victuals, but what such irregular issues may have rendered it, it is not to be conjectured at this distance, wherefore pray please to think whether some present state as it is in *fact* cannot be taken thereof.

Give me leave only to mention the *Gothenburg Convoy* and the two *Swedes* what we are to expect concerning them for the saving time and demurrage.

We have great joy given us from the news of the safety of the *Swiftsure* at the *Nore*, God send it be true.

Your most humble and most faithful servant

S. P.

*Sir W. Coventry*
*June 8th.* 1666.

## LETTER XLVI

¶ This letter reveals some of the consequences of The Four Days' Fight, not only in the demand for masts, mast-makers, sheathing-board and pressed shipwrights, but also in the discontent of the men who, having fought and risked their lives, were paid off with almost worthless tickets.

The *Hind* ketch, mentioned in the postscript, is the vessel in which Pepys took out despatches to Sir Edward Mountagu in the Sound in 1659.

*Sir*

My stay has been so long at *Deptford* to-night to see some things despatched away, that I fear this may come too late to put you in mind of ordering convoy for the Scotch ships by this post.

I have caused another raft of all the great masts we have (and that all is but a little one) at *Deptford* without exception to be made, and will be going down to-morrow, but I am in pain to see what is resolved on, nay and put together to their hands, as several things I did yesterday not sent away to-day, though there be opportunity enough.

I have directed sheathing board to be despatched in *Gibbs's* hoy which goes to-morrow, and given *Sir W. Penn* and *Commissioner Pett* notice thereof, as also told them of what *Masts* are coming and what we have bought of Mr. *Wood*, asking their advice about the working of any of them.

It went out of my head to-day to tell you that I am certainly informed that hundreds of seamen do come daily up to *London* from the fleet. One *gentleman* telling me he overtook yesterday three or four hundred upon the road, I did advertise *Sir W. Penn* of it last night.

*Sir W. Penn* writes to me pressingly for some mast makers and I protest I know not how any can go without much injury to our works here.

I gave my Lord *Brouncker* your advice about closing with the *Alleppin* (?), he was then going with *Grant*

and *Castle* to treat about the fitting of the fire-ships and
told me he would agree for all to-night.

> Your most faithful and most humble servant
>
> *S. P.*

I have set two men at work to-night to press 50 of
*Capt. Taylor's* shipwrights, who will I hope be ready
to go to-morrow evening's tide and (unless you
have cut her out any other work) purpose to send
them down by the *Hinde* ketch.
Would you please that any body may call on
the *Lords Commissioners* for *Prizes* for our
warrant for the two fire-ships.

*Sir W. Coventry*
*June 12th. 1666.*

LETTER XLVII

❡ In spite of the difficulties so well known to all readers of the Diary,
of *Further Correspondence* and these letters, the Navy Board seems
to have supplied the wants of the fleet in less than a month.

*Sir*

In answer to yours of the *26th. which* came last night,
I have only this (which nevertheless will give you I hope
much satisfaction) that *Sir W. Batten* who is at present at
*Deptford* looking to the despatch of some things away to
you, sends me word that of all things both yourself,
*Commissioner Pett,* the storekeeper or Clerk of the *Survey*
of *Chatham* have demanded, nothing will be unsent to-
morrow saving pump chains (of which also about *3 Tons*
as he assures is sent this day) and *Sparrs,* which the
whole town will not furnish us with. *Three* smiths are at
work upon pump chains, to whom we give *40/- per cwt*

ready money (which is a price never yet paid) so that a few days will make up that want too, we hope, and some *porthinges* and *Ringbolts*, in which he tells me we are a little behindhand.

I am glad to see us so near getting over this *brunt* and do heartily wish good success at the end of it, for it's plain we cannot make such another shift as badly as we have done this.

I am Sir

Your most humble servant

*Sir W. Penn*                                     *S. P.*
*and another to Commissioner*
*Pett, mutatis mutandis.*

*June 28th. 1666.*

## LETTER XLVIII      (f. 393)

¶ Pepys was no friend of Sir William Batten and this letter shows him sharing his views on that official with Sir Wm. Coventry. The allusion in the second paragraph is that Batten's private house, 'where he lives like a prince', was at Walthamstow, so that 'setting out towards Harwich' would be a professional euphemism for going home.

*Sir*

Having not your advice, I could the less *urge* to *Sir W. Batten* what my thoughts were of his leaving the office at this *Juncture*, however I did press him as far as became me, but to no purpose, for he's set out toward *Harwich* again now.

I presume nevertheless he means no farther than *Walthamstow*, so that if you yet will please to give me your directions in what I wrote to you this morning, I can if it require me, send to-night to him.

The looking after the demands (which I perceive he

contents himself with leaving to Mr. *Turner*) and the advising us about the disposal of the building of the new ships (which at my entreaty he has left with me in three lines) I do apprehend will much worse spare him than the paying of the yard, where there is a Commissioner and paymaster and what help of clerks shall be thought fit.

 *Sir*

  Your most humble and most affectionate servant

               *S. P.*

Pay each afternoon

*Sir W. Penn* is again now come home and concurs with me herein.

 The *Cartridges* (?) will not be removed till to-morrow.

*Sir W. Coventry*
*July 9th.* 1666.

(f. 401)     MEMORANDUM XLIX

¶ This memorandum occurs after the letter to the Duke of York printed in *Further Correspondence*, pp. 141–2. It supplements the parallel account given in the Diary on 1666 July 26. Sir John Duncombe was Master of the Ordnance. The manœuvre to get the Duke's opinion repeated, so that Batten could hear it, is amusing.

*Memo.* I first showed this this day to *Sir W. Coventry*, who approved of it. Next day we attended the *Duke of York* at *Whitehall* and there I presented it and read it to the *Duke of York* before *Sir G. Carteret, Lord Brouncker, Sir W. Coventry* and *Sir J. Duncombe* and had the *Duke's* good liking of the account I gave, and presently comes in *Sir W. Batten*, so I desired that the *Duke* would let me know whether he was satisfied with the fruit of this experiment in the Victualling business and the charge the King is at. He said "Yes, and I am sure it is much in another condition than it was the last year".

84

¶ It has already been stated that three Capt. Taylors are mentioned in these letters: (*a*) a timber merchant with an unrecorded Christian name, (*b*) Capt. John Taylor, the resident Commissioner at Harwich, whose appointment was referred to in letters Nos. 3, 6 and 24, (*c*) Capt. Silas Taylor, the storekeeper at Harwich, whose appointment is referred to in a letter on p. 85 of *Further Correspondence*. It is supposed that Mr Taylor, the villain of this letter, is Silas, as Pepys would not request Deane to report on his superior after the quarrel and reconciliation already mentioned in the note to letter No. 24. The trouble seems to be in some way connected with the privateer *The Flying Greyhound* which Pepys, Batten and Penn had obtained from the King on the terms stated in this letter. Mr Taylor apparently did not understand the circumstances.

*Mr. Deane*

I thank you heartily for yours of the *27th. Nov.*, and (as there is occasion) continue to give me the like hints for they may be of use to me in informing me in other men's practices, though I hope I shall never need them in reference to any of my own, for you must know that neither the vessel, nor anything else is given us by the King in this matter, but only he is pleased to lend her us and her furniture as also guns etc. during the winter, and we to be accountable for the whole at the end of her voyage. Her victuals we are under contract with *Mr. Gauden* for as private men, and must pay both him and wages and for anything else we spend. This I perceive *Mr. Taylor* do not know, nor let him from you that I may see how he will proceed, for if his observation be on His *Majesty's* behalf, it is commendable in him and I shall do him right in it, but if it be only with a sinister design of laying up something wherewith to charge us, I would be glad to see how far this treacherous mistake will carry him and then get him rewarded, and that I may be better guided in the construction which I am to make of this his deportment, pray give me your observation on him without prejudice how he attends his own duty with what judgment, understanding and diligence, that I may not fall into any ignorant mistake concerning him, though perhaps he may be found guilty of a malicious mistake concerning us.

I am

Your sturdy friend

S. P.

*Navy Office*
*Dec. 1st. 1666.*

(ff. 422–3)

## LETTER LI

¶ It was regarded as an offence to buy seamen's tickets from them at a discount. The last part of the letter shows the alertness of Pepys, whereby £4 a ton was to be saved by forcing a merchant to complete an overlooked contract for hemp.

*Sir*

*By one of the 30th. November from Commissioner Pett (in answer to one from us of the 29th.) he told us he had then taken care for sending the Anchor and Sale demanded by the Colchester into the Downes.*

*The Cable demanded by the Captain of the Harwich wee have ordered to be carryed downe to her hence by the Coronation.*

*The Coulchester's 6 months' victualls was all put on board her at Ipswich. All the Norwich's is loaden away, part soe long since, as might have been with her, and I believe by this time is, the rest had gone this afternoone but for a Lighter which should have brought her and the Colchester's brandy on board her, but being beneaped in St. Saviour's docke could not gett But all wilbe gone to-morrow morneing. Orders are given to Dover to supply them both, soe as to keepe their 6 months' victuals whole.*

*There hath been victualls at Sheerness wherewith to supply the Shipps there these 2 months, and at this time above halfe a score loaden vessells, therefore I can not imagine what the Rupert, Mountagu and Gloucester (which Sir W. Penn mentions from you to-day) should stay for, unless it should be their haveing unmanned the victualling vessells. The last of the Bonaventure's victualling went hence yesterday. I have spoken with the woman you gave me advice of for a Buyer of tickets. She proves an able Citizen's wife, and one who from her readiness to acquainte me with all I had a minde to know I am apt to thinke doth not make it much her Trade. She tells me a poore woman (one Addle) her neighbour came to her with these men, all makeing their moane to her and offering a greater abatement then what she tooke, which (as she saith) was 4 [per cent?] This Addle (she says) had never been with her before, nor since, on this errand. Three or 4 Seamen have been with her since with the like complaints which She hath releaved, but hath since refused wholly others that have come, haveing (as she says) not one of them paid, nor the knowledge of any of our Officers to helpe her, but wishes she might have but her owne money againe for them. This is her Tale, which I shall endeavour to examine the truth of, and see whether this Addle (who was the Brooker) can be made any use of for our inlightening.*

You may please to remember that about 20 days since I acquainted you with a proposition not disliked by you and afterward approved of by the Board, of being served with a ship loading of hemp from *Genoa* at £49 per Ton, on condition of giving the merchant the loan of one of our discharged victualling ships at low price, which proposition from some difficulty made by the owners of the vessels has wanted effect. However it gave us occasion of enquiring into our last year's contract for the same hemp at £45, which not finding performed to the full quantity, the Board directed me to speak with the merchant about it, which I did pressing him to make good the remainder. His defence was chiefly want of [?] to fetch it, which I told him would not excuse it and therefore advised that he should speedily bethink himself of some way of bringing it home. This day he was with me and says if we do resolve to have it, he has treated about a ship, the *Unicorne* of *London*, *Tho. Nun Maister*, of about *120 Tons*, which may be presently fitted to take the advantage of the convoy to *Tangier*, shall go too right to *Genoa*, load and return with as many tons of hemp as that will bring, but prays he may be speedily informed whether we will insist upon having the goods or no, for giving time in fitting the ship if she do go, or know how to put off the master with whom he is in treaty about her in case she do not, this I have promised he shall have to-morrow, whereon I pray your advice.

Your obedient servant

*Sir W. Coventry*
*Dec. 6th. 1666.*

S. P.

(f. 447)                      LETTER LII

¶ Mr Lanyon was the Admiralty agent at Plymouth, the subject of the 'fowle' suggestions in letter No. 54. Lord Ashley, afterwards the first Earl of Shaftesbury, was Chancellor of the Exchequer. The idea was to get some money from the Prize Office, if the Diary entry for 1667 June 5 refers to the same matter. Mr Yeabsly is often mentioned in the Diary, together with Lanyon and Alsopp, in connection with a victualling contract for Tangier.

*Sir*

I have got a bill made out to you for your disbursements on the *Mermayd*. I will endeavour also as soon as

I can to have your other charges allowed, but some of them are such as I cannot so readily judge of.

At your request I shall see how I can make your proposition in your letter of the *15th.* useful to you and thereon do what I am able.

What can be done by my Lord *Ashly* I will try, but it were well I had an abstract of your whole case as to the moneys due to you.

Your answer about the *Nostredame* is well. I am, with respect to Mr. *Yeabsly*

Your affectionate friend to serve you

*S. P.*

*Mr. Lanyon*
*Jan.* 19th. 1666/7

## LETTER LIII                    (f. 447)

¶ This letter is difficult to explain. It is undoubtedly to Commissioner Taylor, but the tone of the letter almost suggests that he was in some new post where his allowances are being enumerated to him. Taylor had, however, been at Harwich for nearly two years and he remained there until 1668 Mar. 25. Letter No. 24 was largely concerned with a suitable house for him.

*Sir*

In answer to yours of the *17th.* inst., when you shall desire it, I presume leave will not be denied you to come up, and truly I doubt it may be but necessary for you, considering the condition the City is in.

I question not but when you shall demand it, an allowance will be made for you for an house, it seeming to me very reasonable.

I have ordered you a bill for the same allowance for pens and paper that Commissioner *Pett* and Commissioner *Middleton* have, which you will receive.

You must inform me whether there be any candles and fire spent for the public use and where, and accordingly I will move for it.

The postage of letters, when you send up an account thereof, will be allowed you. For your servant I will move it seasonably to the Board and speedily give you answer. In the meantime, be confident of all good offices from

Your very faithful friend to serve you

S. P.

*Commissioner Taylor*
*Jan. 19th. 1666/7.*

LETTER LIV

❡ Mr Lanyon has been doing something wrong and is given the advice to prepare his defence. He seems to have been rather unfortunate in this respect, as the following passage concerning him occurs in a letter from Sir Wm. Coventry to Pepys, printed in *Appendix Part II to the Fifteenth Report of the Historical MSS. Commission*:

"1667 Nov. 30, Instance was made of Mr. Lanyon's supplies at Plymouth, with some reflection on him, but vindicated by Sir Fretcheville Holles."

In the Diary for 1668 July 16 there is this passage:

"Up, and to the office, where Yeabsly and Lanyon come to town and to speak with me about a matter wherein they are accused of cheating the King before the Lords Commissioners of Tangier, and I doubt it true, but I have no hand in it, but will serve them what I can."

*Sir*

The *Duke of York* not returning from *Harwich* till Saturday next, I have not had opportunity to move him concerning your *Purchase-mony*, but will do it speedily after his return and in the best manner I can.

I do think it may be convenient for me to tell you that I had yesterday a hint given me of an intention to have a person sent down to *Plymouth* in quality of a commissioner and that it will be *Sir T. Allen.* The occasion of it is that we shall have a considerable squadron of ships to the *Westward* all this year, which he is to have the directing of, and to the purpose to reside at *Plymouth.* It is yet a secret, so that I cannot tell you more particulars, but I did think it would be useful to you to know thus much.

There is another thing which I am sure do much concern you to know and remedy. It is this. *Mr. Waltham* has this week informed us that you complained of want of supplies for several things, although you have received from the boatswain and other officers sails, rigging and else to furnish your own ships, and that you will give him no account of *Credit* for it without our order, pretending what is received from the several ships is in lieu of what you have delivered to the said frigate and rated as new from the *Ropes* and others which is otherwise he is informed by the officers of the ships.

This service I have done you to prevent the Board's being precipitated into a bad opinion of you till at the same time your defence were ready, but the things which he suggests are so *fowle,* that as they cannot be concealed so neither ought they be true, nor will any friend appear in your excuse when any of this shall be proved, therefore pray make a fit use of this advertisement without any words to Mr. *Waltham* (who will be [owned?] in any just complaints) and let me have your answer hereto by the next.

I am

Your truly faithful friend to serve you

*Mr. Lanyon*                                              *S. P.*
*March 21st. 1666/7*

¶ This undated memorandum concerning the Dutch Invasion of the Medway is between two letters each dated 1667 June 11. Pepys went down to Gravesend on June 10 and his letter to Sir Wm. Coventry giving an account of what he did and saw is printed in *Further Correspondence*, pp. 176–7. The *Little Mary* had been captured by the Dutch in 1666 Oct. while engaged in protecting the fishing fleet off Yarmouth. (*Cal. S. P. Dom.*) Lord Wor— may well be Lord Worcester, who succeeded to that title in April 1667, thus satisfying the statement 'that now is'. 'The silly Duke of Albemarle' expresses Pepys' normal opinion of him. In the Diary on 1667 Dec. 27 he is the object of the following:

"Which is an odd consideration for a dull, heavy blockhead as he is, understanding no more of either than a goose."

*For my owne memory I adde* in this book

These *Dutch* ships came thither last night. That they were repelled from *Lee* by the care of one *Justice Hare*. That they took a small fisher smack and put some men into her and they did this mischief. That the orders of our four ships that are in the Hope, the *Success, Diamond, Portland and Reserve* did go off thinking to have intercepted her in her return, but being sped or prevented by a fire-ship of the Dutch\*, who weighed and came and did give them a broadside. This fire-ship they think to be our Little Mary\* that was taken from us, or the *Merlin*. I thought the *Block-house* a most contemptible place, and a great many idle gentlemen and Lords, among other *Lord Wor*— that now is, and *Carlisle* and others came thither with their pistols and lackeys and I know not who, and the silly *Duke of Albemarle*, but it was methought a sorry thing that they should in this time stand all hearing of the guns play below. I know they were gone down as low as *Sheerness* and yet not go to *Chatham*, nor send but considered of fortifying this place by ships being brought up thither.

* Shorthand.

My attendance here has hindered my waiting on you for these two or three days to give you, an account first touching the payment of standing officers (*viz*. the purser, boatswain, gunner and carpenter) not ever being made by ticket (by reason of the time necessary after the ship's coming in to pass their accounts) unless where by accident through the want of money the ship lies long in harbour undischarged, in these cases (which are rare) some have been paid with the rest of the company. The *Cook* as being accountable for nothing, is paid by book.

I have one at work on the other business, concerning which I hope to give you speedy answer.

Honoured *Sir*

Your most obedient servant

*S. P.*

*Sir W. Coventry*
*March* 30*th.* 1668.

# APPENDIX

## LETTER LVII

❡ The following letter is in longhand throughout, but a few passages are in a numerical cipher. As the amount of ciphered material is very small, it was thought at one time that it would be quite impossible to decipher it, until I learned, by chance, that the key to the cipher is preserved in the Bodleian Library. Mr O. E. Holloway has again favoured me by looking out the meanings of the ciphered passage and the letter is now given in full. In this one case, italics represent the ciphered passages. The 'Addresse of this day's Date', referred to in the last paragraph, is undoubtedly the letter recommending Daniel Skinner, which is printed in *Letters and the Second Diary of Samuel Pepys*, p. 56.

Derby House, 24th. July 1676

My Lord,

Since that wherein I rendred your Excellency my humble thanks for the honour of yours by which you were pleased to lodge with mee the Account of what befell His Majesty's Yacht the Charles in her Rencounter with the States man of War in the River of the Brill and wherein I also adventur'd to trouble your Excellency with a *mournful* line or two *in cipher* upon occasion of some earlier intimations I had of what is since become *matter of more publique knowledge and desperation*, I mean, *the Duke of York his open declaring himself a papist*, I have taken too little Satisfaction in any thing that has since occurr'd that I should encrease your other Sufficient Solicitudes with any part thereof.

I am now to acknowledge the honour of yours of the 24th. of the last, of which I shall not faile to make the

94

timeliest and most effectual use I can towards the obtaining right, not only to the two Gentlemen you mention, with particular regard to your owne Honourable Office in the Admiralty, but (in them) to the King and Government also in providing for the support of that Discipline, which (as your selfe are pleased rightly to observe) must suffer where its Ministers are not equally provided for; nor doe I despair of being enabled in a little time from the justice of His Majesty and His Royal Highness' mediation to give you some good account of the matter with the help of the Inducements you have been pleas'd to furnish me with towards it.

What I have to add is, the telling you that I have taken the liberty of becoming a Suitor to your Excellency by a particular Addresse of this day's Date which will be conveyed to you by the care of the Party interested: for which begging Your Excellency's Pardon and with most faithful Professions and Service and Honour to your Excellency I remaine

    My Lord

Your Excellency's most devoted and obedient Servant

                          S. P.

His Excellency Sir Leoline Jenkins
Embassador Extra from
His Majesty of Great Britaine
at Nimegues.

# INDEX

For EU product safety concerns, contact us at Calle de José Abascal, 56–1°,
28003 Madrid, Spain or eugpsr@cambridge.org.

www.ingramcontent.com/pod-product-compliance
Ingram Content Group UK Ltd.
Pitfield, Milton Keynes, MK11 3LW, UK
UKHW012334130625
459647UK00009B/280